OFF THE MAIN LINES

RAILROADS PAST & PRESENT   *George M. Smerk, editor*

A list of books in the series appears at the end of this volume.

INDIANA UNIVERSITY PRESS   *Bloomington & Indianapolis*

Off the Main Lines

A Photographic Odyssey   DON L. HOFSOMMER

This book is a publication of

INDIANA UNIVERSITY PRESS
Office of Scholarly Publishing
Herman B Wells Library 350
1320 E. 10th Street
Bloomington, Indiana 47405 USA

iupress.indiana.edu

Telephone orders 800-842-6796
Fax orders 812-855-7931

© 2013 by Donovan L. Hofsommer

⊗ The paper used in this publication meets the minimum requirements of the American National Standard for Information Sciences – Permanence of Paper for Printed Library Materials, ANSI Z39.48–1992.

Manufactured in South Korea

*Library of Congress
Cataloging-in-Publication Data*

Hofsommer, Donovan L.
  Off the main lines : a photographic odyssey / Don L. Hofsommer.
    p. cm. – (Railroads past and present)
  Includes bibliographic references and index.
  ISBN 978-0-253-00832-9 (pb : alk. paper) – ISBN 978-0-253-00868-8 (eb) 1. Narrow gauge railroads – West (U.S.) – History. 2. Narrow gauge railroads – Colorado – History. 3. Narrow gauge railroads – Colorado – Pictorial works. 4. Narrow gauge railroads – West (U.S.) – Pictorial works.
  I. Title. II. Series: Railroads past and present.
  TF23.6.H64 2013
  385.0978 – dc23

                                        2012047304

1 2 3 4 5   18 17 16 15 14 13

FOR DAD AND HIS GRANDSON,
VERNIE AND KNUTE

CONTENTS

OFF THE MAIN LINES

MY STEEL-TRAIL ODYSSEY BEGAN AT CALLENDER, A small central Iowa village on Minneapolis & St. Louis's (M&StL) Minneapolis–Albert Lea–Fort Dodge–Des Moines line, where my father managed the yard at S. Hanson Lumber Company, a vibrant place during the late 1930s and early 1940s when that rural, agrarian portion of the country finally threw off the dread yoke of the Depression.

Dad and his hired hands unloaded lump coal arriving in gondola cars from mines in Illinois and Kentucky, dimension and finish lumber in boxcars from Pacific Northwest origins, posts in gondolas from northern Minnesota, asphalt shingles in boxcars from manufacturers at Kansas City, bagged cement in boxcars from West Des Moines, and plaster in boxcars from nearby Fort Dodge. M&StL also delivered less-than-carload (LCL) freight in the form of one-hundred-pound kegs of nails, millwork, and hardware in abundant variety. Other small shipments arrived by Brady Motor Freight, and local truckers hauled in clay products from brick and tile works at Kalo and Lehigh. In all, the lumberyard was a busy and exciting place, the alley of the yard humming with deliveries and the comings and goings of customers.

Up the track was Callender Grain's "north elevator" and bulk plants, where tank cars of kerosene and gasoline were unloaded and contents stored and eventually distributed to the town's two filling stations, Standard Oil and Sovereign Service, and to area farmsteads. M&StL's pens and chutes handled occasional livestock billings.

Down the track stood the "middle elevator" and the "south elevator," the latter with Callender Grain's office and the cigar-loving and always affable Frank Peterson, manager. Trailers drawn by teams of horses or by tractors and trucks brought in prodigious harvests of corn, oats, and soybeans that in due course were disgorged from elevator bins, dribbling down spouts into waiting coopered boxcars bound for a variety of destinations.

M&StL's sober-looking depot was the fulcrum of Callender's "metropolitan corridor." Gregarious and talented Clifford K. Ferguson was the monarch there, and also the town's mayor, until promotion into sales at Peoria, where over the next two decades he drummed up business for M&StL. O. M. Olson followed, but he, too, was promoted and left to become a dispatcher at Cedar Lake (Minneapolis). No matter the personage,

Callender's "depot agent" was "somebody." And although the full-blown age of railways may have passed, these were the early years of World War II with rationing of tires and gasoline, with the depot regaining community centrality as a consequence.

The agent's office was a tobacco-smelling place with a pot-bellied stove and a built-in table-desk stretching from one side of the trackside bay to the other. On that table were telegraph instruments, a lever governing the outside train-order signal, and shelves for train order forms, etc. The room likewise featured a captain's chair with glass insulators for the agent; a straight chair without insulators; an office desk; jars of vitriol associated with the telegraph; a wall clock; a small safe; a ticket case; a ticket dater; a tariff case with various rate books, lanterns, and flags; train-order hoops; a brass wax sealer and banker's wax; a copy of the *Official Guide of the Railways;* and a broom, shovel, coal bucket, and duster. On the north wall hung an M&StL calendar with the image of an onrushing, modernized Mikado heading a long train of freight cars to assert the road's robust vitality.

The freight house was dark, dirty, and a bit spooky. It was locked from the outside except when opened by the agent to meet the needs of patrons, by the local mail messenger, or by trainmen. Inside were sundry items: banana or bread boxes, crates of cheeping baby chicks or mature poultry, mail, baggage, express, and LCL freight including everything from caskets to corsets.

A daily parade of people flowed to and from the depot. Section men stopped in to get "line ups," to eat their lunches in the waiting room, or to lounge a few minutes late in the day before "quittin' time." Freight customers popped in and out with bills of lading or to pick up or ship LCL or express. Others drifted in to send or receive telegrams, to purchase tickets, or simply to kibitz with the agent. M&StL operated its regularly scheduled trains at night and the agent went off duty late in the afternoon, but that only added to the depot's intrigue. The northbound passenger train was scheduled for around 10:30 PM, and especially in summer months, a congregation of locals appeared to witness that seminal event in the town's life. To pass time prior to the train's arrival, one could press an ear to the single-pane bay window and hear the faint clatter of the relay telegraph instruments, their magic utterly captivating and bewildering to the uninitiated.

During winter months, Dad periodically needed to be in Des Moines, and in a few instances, Mom and I went along on the southbound train. The depot took on a totally different atmosphere in the dead of night, about 4 AM, as we sat on hard benches in the waiting room, with Dad poking at the dull remnants of a fire in the large potbellied stove, throwing on a lump or two of coal in faint hope of driving chill from the room. There was no operator on duty, of course, but the door to the waiting room was left open, and patrons were free to turn on the light, a bulb on a long cord suspended from the ceiling, and rebuild the fire, or not, as they saw fit. On the north wall next to the agent's office was a board with the schedule of arrivals chalked in. On the west wall was a government poster admonishing us that, because this was wartime, we should not discuss train movements ("Shhh, the enemy might be listening"). Next to it was another poster asking if this trip was necessary; after all, troops had first lien on passenger service. And another urgently pointed out that "USA Has Right Of Way – Motorists Must Wait" at grade crossings so that impedimenta of war could move expeditiously along the nation's rail arteries. Yet another urged the purchase of war bonds as a "Highball to Victory."

All of it reflected a routine typical of small communities across the land at a time when railroads still set the tempo of life.

I was exposed early to the excitement of Callender's metropolitan corridor and particularly to its spine, the railway. That virus took deep root. Indeed, I never got over it.

Dad inadvertently abetted this malady by allowing me to prowl around the lumberyard and occasionally go with him on errands to the depot. I was firmly instructed not to go there by myself, but I did not always obey; there were ways to subvert his intent. I learned, for instance, that Iva Hansen, Callender's postmaster, wheeled the day's mail to the freight house after closing her office. Surprise! I became her attendant. And I tagged along with Paul Dallman, the section boss from Gowrie, when he went to the depot on company business or merely to chew the fat with the agent.

Dallman was one of three brothers who became section foremen at M&StL. He and his crew handled the track maintenance through Callender and were well-known local fixtures. One day, Dallman told me that the "weed burner" soon was expected. Would I like to be with him as the gang "scorched" the line through Callender? Does a bear like honey?

Wage controls during the war prevented Hanson Lumber from giving my father the increase he thought he deserved, but such restrictions did not apply to commissions. That led him to become an insurance agent. The change in his occupation led us in 1944 to Fort Dodge, the capital of Webster County, Iowa, not far away, and to a home on the north edge of the city hard by M&StL's Albert Lea–Fort Dodge artery. Also in the city were Illinois Central (IC), Chicago Great Western (CGW or Great Western), and electrified Fort Dodge, Des Moines & Southern (FtDDM&S or Fort Dodge Line). So far as I was concerned, Fort Dodge was the railroad center of the universe. It was while residing there that I came into possession of a camera, a Brownie 127 I exercised in a totally unsophisticated program of "point and click." I also discovered *Trains Magazine* in the rack of a local drug store.

An improved business opportunity for Dad in 1948 took us to Spencer, in northwest Iowa, served by M&StL's Fort Dodge–Spencer–Estherville route, and by two Chicago, Milwaukee, St. Paul & Pacific (CMStP&P or Milwaukee Road) lines: Chicago–Mason City–Rapid City, Iowa & Dakota (I&D) Division, and Des Moines–Spencer–Spirit Lake, Iowa Division. There were ample opportunities to utilize my plastic Brownie, then 116 and 130 folding cameras, and finally a 2¼ × 3¼ Graflex.

It was off to school in 1956, to Iowa State Teachers College at Cedar Falls, a place graced by IC; Great Western; Chicago, Rock Island & Pacific (CRI&P or Rock Island); and electrified Waterloo, Cedar Falls & Northern (WCF&N). A student-teaching assignment early in 1960 led me to Mason City, another railroad-rich community featuring M&StL; Great Western; Rock Island; Milwaukee Road; Chicago & North Western (C&NW or North Western); and electrified Mason City & Clear Lake (MC&CL).

A stint in the army and a taste of graduate school preceded a teaching job at Fairfield, in southeast Iowa and junction point of Chicago, Burlington & Quincy's (CB&Q or Burlington Route) busy Chicago–Omaha–Denver main and Rock Island's Chicago–Kansas City–Santa Rosa Golden State Route. Fairfield also introduced me to Sandra, the wonderful and tolerant woman who became my wife in 1964 and whom I dragged off to a "graduate school honeymoon" at Adams State College in – where else – Alamosa, Colorado, eastern terminus of Denver & Rio Grande Western's (D&RGW or Rio Grande) remaining narrow-gauge empire. Adams professors were competent and demanding, but time was adequate to explore the wonders of the Colorado narrow gauge.

A year of graduate school, 1965–66, to complete a master's degree at Cedar Falls, was followed by four years of teaching at Lea College in Albert Lea, Minnesota. Here was the former M&StL Minneapolis–Peoria main as well as the line to Fort Dodge and Des Moines; Rock Island's Minneapolis–Des Moines–Kansas City Mid-Continent Route, with a branch to Estherville, Iowa; an IC line to Waterloo, Iowa; and Milwaukee Road's southern Minnesota artery into South Dakota, with a spur to St. Clair. The Lea experience also included two summers of graduate work at the University of Montana at Missoula, on the transcontinental lines of both Northern Pacific (NP) and Milwaukee Road.

Change was afoot. The railroad industry was in a deepening malaise that was reflected locally; none of the four roads at Albert Lea was robust and, although we did not discern it at the moment, Milwaukee Road and Rock Island were on a collision course with oblivion. Change was in the offing for my wife and I, too, as in 1970 we simultaneously became parents and pushed off to Stillwater, Oklahoma, and a PhD program at Oklahoma State University, where I was able to complete a dissertation on the birth, life, and death of Missouri–Kansas–Texas's (M–K–T or Katy) Northwestern District.

Then it was on to jobs at Plainview, Texas, south of Amarillo and north of Lubbock, Atchison, Topeka & Santa Fe country (AT&SF or Santa Fe) but shared with Fort Worth &

Denver (FW&D). And nearby was Quanah, Acme & Pacific (QA&P), which offered a new research opportunity.

A most pleasurable assignment with Southern Pacific (SP) and subsequently helping Burlington Northern (BN) finish up a long-delayed Great Northern book was followed by my return to higher education and an administrative position at Augustana College in Sioux Falls, South Dakota. Later, I returned to teaching at St. Cloud State University in Minnesota.

:   :   :

Our sojourn over these years has taken us to several locations in the heartland, some of them on main lines, others served only by humble branches. And over these same years, considerable change has surrounded the railroad industry, including the transition from steam to diesel, the demise of electric roads, the end of branch-line passenger service and eventually loss of passenger operation by investor-owned carriers, massive abandonment of branches and even main lines, mergers and consolidations, deregulation, resurgence, explosion of unit trains, and startling growth of intermodal business.

I tried to record some of this evolution on film, especially at lesser known places from Callender, Iowa, to Roaring Springs, Texas. The pages following comprise an illustrated representation of an excursion principally away from main routes but rather along branches and secondary lines, loosely defined as unsignaled or "dark" territory. It's been fun.

All aboard!

The steam-car civilization came to Callender, Iowa, in the fall of 1870 when Des Moines Valley (DMV) pushed its existing line from Keokuk to Des Moines northwestward from Iowa's capital city through Perry to Fort Dodge. Kesho, the original townsite, simply picked up and moved across the tracks to the west and rechristened itself Callender. Early train service included a through-passenger run from Keokuk plus scheduled freights.

Des Moines Valley unfortunately was unhealthy. Out of it in 1874 came two roads: Keokuk & Des Moines (K&D), which inherited DMV's avenue between those points, and Des Moines & Fort Dodge (DM&FtD), which acquired the northern section through Callender. DM&FtD advertised itself as "The Fort Dodge Route – The Great Throughfare between Des Moines and the North and Northwest." Heady stuff that, but, in fact, the company was no more robust than DMV, its predecessor. Giant Chicago, Rock Island & Pacific (Rock Island) took lease of it in 1887, the lease in 1905 passing to Minneapolis & St. Louis (M&StL), which some years later bought the property.

M&StL itself was hardly robust and nearly devoid of baubles and cotillions. It slumped into receivership in 1923 and in the next decade barely avoided dismemberment in a way that would have left Callender devoid of rail service. The railroad patched and scrimped, however, economizing as best it could. Ministrations of Lucian C. Sprague and an improved economy eventually saved it. Out of receivership in 1943, the company was without bonded debt. Sprague announced that M&StL no longer stood for "Misery & Short Life," but, rather, "Modern & Streamlined." The Sprague management fell to outside raiders in 1954, and that, in turn, set up sale of the road to Chicago & North Western (C&NW) six years later.

Train operation on the line during our time at Callender was at best humble – one passenger train and one freight train in each direction per day, all at night, plus an occasional troop train or an extra freight. Gas–electric cars trailed one or two weary storage mail cars and a venerable coach on the Minneapolis–Albert Lea–Fort Dodge–Des Moines passenger run. Consolidation (2–8–0) steam locomotives drew the Fort Dodge–Des Moines freights.

M&StL for me was the "home road." And it always would be.

The depot at Callender by 1963, when this view was made, was tattered. It would only get worse. Indeed, its glory years, when it served very clearly as the community pivot, were well passed. But what glory years they had been.

In 1949, M&StL shifted its Minneapolis–Des Moines passenger schedule from night to day. Train 1, up from Des Moines, pauses at Callender at 10:30 on this warm summer morning in 1950.

Callender was one of forty-four station stops for train 2 on its daily 299-mile trek from Minneapolis to Des Moines. Agent Earl L. Lund doubled as mail messenger, moving pouches, sacks, and parcels to and from the post office. The S. Hanson lumberyard is out of sight to the left of the depot. The north elevator and bulk plants are seen along the house track in the background. Summer 1950.

Train 2, heading for Des Moines, rolls past Callender Grain's south elevator, where Frank Peterson was manager and where Paul Dallman and his section gang killed time on occasion. Earlier in the day, corn had rattled down the elevator's spout to fill boxcars on the house track. Note the stacks of boards for grain doors necessary in coopering the cars. Summer 1950.

Train 2, headed by GE-27 and now powered by a Caterpillar D-397 engine, purrs over a well-groomed if lightly ballasted track south of Callender on an idyllic day in August 1954. The rich soil of the area promised bountiful agricultural tonnage for M&StL.

If Minneapolis & St. Louis was for me the home road, Chicago, Rock Island & Pacific was the ancestral taproot.

Rock Island was, as Huddie "Leadbelly" Ledbetter so aptly put it, "a mighty fine line." It brought to Iowa and gave utility to all four of my grandparents, those on my father's side settling at Dysart and those on my mother's side locating at Dows, both stations on Rock Island's southeast–northwest artery across the state. Other relatives of my father migrated farther up the line to take residency at Trosky, Minnesota, and in the 1920s, Rock Island provided transportation for Dad and other members of the Dows High School team to wrestling matches at other towns.

My own life had corresponding ties to the "mighty fine line."

I warmly recall standing in or near Grandfather Lars Schager's barn southeast of Dows at evening milking time, gazing across open fields at train 20, a three-car passenger train headed by a strange-looking power unit that burbled and gurbled its way through the night toward Cedar Rapids. In later years, I rode that train and looked across those same fields to the Schager place, imagining that Grandpa was looking back at me.

Rock Island's line through Dysart, Dows, and Trosky was completed by Burlington, Cedar Rapids & Northern (BCR&N) and associates in bits and pieces during the years 1873–84 and was operated as BCR&N's Pacific Division. Indeed, when Rock Island gained control of BCR&N, and M&StL briefly, as well, it did have aspirations of making good on the "Pacific" in its corporate title by way of a northwest passage. That did not happen, of course, but this part of BCR&N did provide a wonderfully rich source of traffic. Rock Island purchased BCR&N outright in 1903.

At the outset of World War II, Rock Island scheduled a daily "passenger motor" and one freight in each direction through Dows on the Cedar Rapids–Sioux Falls run, plus a daily-except-Sunday mixed from Iowa Falls through Dows and then up a spur to Belmond and Garner to Lakota. The passenger was trimmed back from Sioux Falls to Estherville in 1950 and eliminated altogether in 1956. In 1950 and for several years thereafter, the mixed to Lakota originated and terminated at Dows.

In time, the "mighty fine line" stumbled and fell, sad to say. Other roads picked at the carcass. C&NW took what it wanted, including portions of the former BCR&N, like the line through Dows. Then, in a monumental strategic blunder, C&NW abandoned the portion from Dows through Popejoy and Burdette to Iowa Falls.

The standpipe at Dows was little used when this autumnal view was made in 1951. But CRI&P maintained water facilities there even after steam disappeared so that hogs moving in carload lots (likely to slaughter at the huge Wilson & Company packing plant in Cedar Rapids) could be showered and cooled on the hot and humid days of summer. The combine at right was assigned to mixed-train duty on the seventy-one-mile branch from Dows through Garner to Lakota. No. 20 on this day is a bit off the advertised schedule, due out 5:37 PM but actually departing at 5:51. In a few minutes, it will pass in sight of the Schager farmstead southeast of town.

Motor 9007 began life as a humble mail car, but an enterprising Rock Island in 1937 converted it into a gas–electric unit that was dieselized three years later to produce 800 horsepower. On February 21, 1954, it put in a familiar appearance on train 20 near Graettinger, Iowa. Rock Island in 1950 had suspended passenger service above Estherville to Sioux Falls, South Dakota, but trains 19 and 20 still offered connections by way of the *Zephyr–Rocket* at Cedar Rapids to and from Chicago (via West Liberty) and St. Louis.

Rock Island's financial fortunes were as
dreary as the weather on this raw February
day in 1970 when this drag rumbled through
Dows. The impressive depot structure
later became an Iowa Welcome Center.

FORT DODGE, IOWA: CENTER OF
THE RAILROAD UNIVERSE

Iowa predecessors of Illinois Central (IC) in 1869 completed a line from Dubuque to Fort Dodge, pushing westward a year later to link Sioux City, in that way structuring an important horizontal thoroughfare from the Mississippi River to the Missouri. Later on, affiliates fleshed it out with a line from Cherokee to Sioux Falls, South Dakota, and another southwestward from Cherokee to Onawa. The western-Iowa system was rounded out at century's end with a strategic arm from Tara, just west of Fort Dodge, to Council Bluffs and Omaha. IC's flagship passenger train was the overnight *Hawkeye,* heavy with "head-end" cars of mail, express, and baggage as well as coaches and sleepers. The *Iowan* handled daylight chores until it was discontinued in 1949–50. Freights, especially time freights (IC dispatch trains) proliferated. IC was the premier handler of meat and packing-house products across Iowa billed from on-line plants like Tobin at Fort Dodge, and it likewise wheeled huge volumes of "green freight" (perishables, fruits and vegetables) received at Council Bluffs from Union Pacific (UP), with these trains often running in multiple sections. Among Fort Dodge railroads, IC was the only one signaled, with ABS (automatic block signal), but only up the hill to Tara and to the east. It changed crews at Fort Dodge and boasted a large engine facility and impressive depots for passengers and freight.

DM&FtD reached the latter place in 1870 from Des Moines, Iowa's capital; it passed to control of M&StL in 1905. M&StL itself completed a route to Fort Dodge from Minneapolis and Albert Lea in 1881, pushing on to the south for the purpose of reaching coalfields at Kalo and Angus during the next season. By the mid-1940s, M&StL's passenger service was down to a nightly train in each direction from Minneapolis to Des Moines and another between Fort Dodge and Winthrop, Minnesota. Freights were made up in the yard for Des Moines, Albert Lea, and Spencer. Crews changed at Fort Dodge, the road sported an ice facility to protect perishable lading, and locomotives were serviced at a ramshackle roundhouse. M&StL used IC's passenger station.

Chicago Great Western (CGW) predecessor Mason City & Fort Dodge (MC&FtD) connected those two communities in 1886, and in 1903, CGW forged its own route from Fort Dodge to Council Bluffs. Its stub-end passenger facility was at the eastern boundary of downtown. Crews changed elsewhere, and CGW had only abbreviated yard facilities. In 1947, CGW carded double-daily passenger operation on its Minneapolis–Omaha line through Fort Dodge, along with two two-time freights and one local in each direction. A special feature was CGW's very substantial bridge over IC, M&StL, and the Des Moines River.

Fort Dodge, Des Moines & Southern (Fort Dodge Line) was the latecomer. By construction on its own and by acquisition of existing properties, a new route linking Fort Dodge and Des Moines was cobbled together in 1907. Fort Dodge Line later added a line eastward to Lehigh and Webster City. Electrification followed. In 1948, it scheduled four daily passenger runs from Fort Dodge to Des Moines, with freights operating for the most part at night.

During the mid-1940s it was virtually impossible to be outside at Fort Dodge and not hear whistles, bells, or engine exhaust from some part of town. IC was majordomo, all steam with the most melodic of steamboat whistles, Pacifics and occasionally a Mountain on passenger assignments, Mikados and Mountains on freights, with barrel-chested 0–8–0s and perky 0–6–0s in switching and helper service.

M&StL featured gas–electric cars on passenger runs, 2–8–0s on freights, a diminutive General Electric switcher that exposed the city to the forthcoming era of dieselization, and an 0–6–0 held in reserve. CGW used 4–6–0s and 4–6–2s on passenger runs, with 2–8–2s assigned to freight. Single cars normally were adequate on Fort Dodge Line passenger runs, although there were times when demand required cars in multiple, while freight motors handled switching duties and the usually scheduled nocturnal drags.

Illinois Central was majordomo at Fort Dodge. Crews changed there, as did locomotives, except passenger power. IC's roundhouse-service facility was a busy place as a result. A 1500-class Mikado with auxiliary tank has arrived with a drag from the west and awaits attention. The steam-powered clamshell at right served to clean the ash pits. IC's substantial freight house looms in the background. April 11, 1952.

In early 1952, IC still dispatched its road trains to and through Fort Dodge with steam power, but diesel switchers like 9420 supplanted the usual 0–6–0s and 0–8–0s that increasingly found themselves slumbering in the roundhouse. Late in the afternoon of February 10, the nearly new diesel lines up with 2–8–2s 1501 and 1557 resting together.

Mikados like Lima-built 1534 were ubiquitous. On this October day in 1952, it would wheel train 75 (Dispatch CC3) on the 136-mile dash from Fort Dodge to Council Bluffs, replacing a 4–8–2 that brought the train from Waterloo.

Diesels soon would end the reign of 4–6–2s and 4–8–2s on the *Hawkeye*, **but on March 27, 1954, Mountain 2401 had the honors.** The train would make eleven station stops west of Fort Dodge before completing its run from Chicago to Sioux City.

By the late 1960s, Geeps and E-units alternated as power on trains 11 and 12, the *Hawkeye*, but the evening routine for the eastbound run remained the same at Fort Dodge: a fifteen-minute pause to unload and load passengers, mail, express, and baggage. July 1969.

Clerks in the Railway Mail Service were admonished: "Do not delay baby chicks or the *Wall Street Journal*." Shipments from the Welp Hatchery at Bancroft head east on Chicago & Fort Dodge RPO 12. July 1969.

General Electric's forty-four-ton D-842 often found yard duty for M&StL at Fort Dodge. At left is one of the road's Russell snowplows, to the right, one of its Alco road switchers with Chicago Great Western's impressive bridge in the background. November 6, 1952.

Alco 1,000 hp road switchers held all M&StL freight assignments at Fort Dodge during the first half of the 1950s. Four of them (one is hidden) await calls on the north side of the ramshackle roundhouse on a sparkling June morning in 1951. In the background at left is cGW's substantial bridge over ic, M&StL, and the Des Moines River.

M&StL held trackage rights over Illinois Central between Tara and Fort Dodge, five miles. Here, train 1 hustles east, away from Tara, downgrade into the Des Moines River Valley at Fort Dodge. August 1952.

Since 1901, M&StL had utilized IC's impressive passenger facility at Fort Dodge. Up from Des Moines en route to Minneapolis, train 1 warms in unseasonable sun on February 10, 1952.

In 1948, M&StL purchased elegant stainless steel coaches that bobbed incongruously behind its venerable **GE cars.** On May 15, 1954, GE-26 heads train 1 up the valley of Soldier Creek (*above*) and out of Fort Dodge (*overleaf*).

In the days of steam, northbound M&StL freights often required a helper up the hill out of Fort Dodge, and on this May day in 1954, Alco 1050 has its hands full with a heavy train 51, headed for Albert Lea, Minnesota.

This August day of 1954 was steamy and hot, but passengers enjoyed air-conditioned comfort in the coach trailing **GE-27.** Train 2, south of Badger, is about to roll down the valley into Fort Dodge.

Chicago Great Western's double-daily passenger service at Fort Dodge in 1948 included the *Twin Cities Express,* up from Omaha to St. Paul and Minneapolis on a daylight schedule. It backed into the Central Avenue station to exchange passengers, mail, express, and baggage late in the noon hour. The stop was adequate for Engineer Herbert B. Fuller to "oil" the moving parts of his iron steed and take up conversation with the young kid who seemed to show up automatically at train time during the summer. And it was the kind and generous Fuller who brought that kid passenger timetables he had gathered up at the ticket windows of the Burlington and Union stations in Omaha before he headed his train out of town. July 1948.

Brakeman B. W. "Barney" Bird drops off the locomotive, and a carman crouches to inspect train 50 as it eases into the Fort Dodge Yard to complete its trip from Albert Lea. January 1961.

CGW was fully dieselized by November 30, 1952, when this Alco road switcher on the freight turn from Clarion performed yard work at Fort Dodge.

Wartime demand for passenger transportation caused Fort Dodge, Des Moines & Southern to schedule four daily runs on its eighty-five-mile route between Fort Dodge and Des Moines. That pattern obtained after the war, too, but by 1951, that service was halved. Car 74 waits at the Fort Dodge terminal on May 10, 1953, for the afternoon trip to Iowa's capital city. In the background is the loop track to turn the cars.

The afternoon car for Des Moines departed at 4:10 on April 11, 1953.

Shadows were lengthening for FtDDM&S passenger service on
this splendid May day in 1954 when car 82 with train 4 eased
up and out of the Des Moines River Valley near Shady Oak.

With passengers and mail aboard, veteran and well-known Conductor Albert P. Butts could get on with his bookwork. The run to Des Moines took two hours and forty minutes with a ride that was as much up and down and side to side as it was forward. Visitors often found themselves up front with the motorman.

One or both of the two four-motor, eighty-ton giants slumbering in the East Fort Dodge Yard on February 10, 1952, would likely head for Boone and Des Moines after dark on routine freight assignments.

FtDDM&S dieselized in 1953–55, principally with seventy-ton units from General Electric that could be run in multiple for freight service or singly as switchers. East Fort Dodge, February 1963.

Milwaukee Road's *Sioux*, west of Mason City, typically drew F-5 4–6–2s; 802, as on this day in November 1951, was a frequent visitor, as was 817. This routine was altered very briefly in the spring of 1950 when CMStP&P dispatched F-6 4–6–4 monsters bumped from main-line runs by diesels. They caused a major stir, especially among locals who regularly congregated at the Grand Avenue depot in the early evening "at train time" to post letters on the RPO car, watch enginemen shake the grates, see the engineer "oil around," the fireman "take water" in the tender, or simply absorb the excitement and frenetic energy surrounding the passage of the eastbound *Sioux*, train 22. In any event, F-6 125 and 127 ventured out on the I&D Division for only a few trips because rumor had them too heavy for bridges. F-5s returned briefly, and then they, too, disappeared in favor of diesels, though one F-5 stayed in the roundhouse at Mason City into 1953 as protection power for the *Sioux*).

Railroad construction across the country surged after the Panic of 1873. Part of this was reflected in Iowa by a major artery across the northern part of the state started earlier from the Mississippi River at Marquette and subsequently acquired by Chicago, Milwaukee & St. Paul (CM&StP) (later Chicago, Milwaukee, St. Paul & Pacific). Stalled by the Panic at Algona and awaiting a positive shift in the land–man ratio to the west, crews did not renew their labors until 1878, pushing then through Spencer and on into Dakota Territory. Spencer was not made a crew-change point, but in 1882–83, Milwaukee Road drove a spur northward into the lakes region of adjoining Dickinson County to serve Arnolds Park, Okoboji, and Spirit Lake. Toward the end of the century, CM&StP acquired an existing line from Des Moines to Fonda and in 1899 extended it from Fonda to Spencer, linking there with the Spirit Lake branch to forge a direct diagonal route from the capital city to the resort area of northwest Iowa. In 1948, the *Sioux* offered daily passenger service in each direction between Chicago and Rapid City, with a heavy complement of mail, express, and baggage cars, plus coaches, sleepers, and a café–observation car. The *Sioux* shared operation through Spencer on the Iowa & Dakota (I&D) Division with two daily time freights and a way freight in each direction. The Iowa Division featured a daily-except-Sunday Des Moines–Spirit Lake passenger train and a daily-except-Sunday freight in each direction between Perry and Spirit Lake. Milwaukee Road at Spencer also garrisoned a locomotive and crew assigned the "Spencer Patrol" to perform local switching chores and runs to nearby stations as required.

Minneapolis & St. Louis entered the scene in 1900 with a north–south route from Winthrop, Minnesota, connecting to Minneapolis, through New Ulm and Estherville and on through Spencer to Storm Lake. After M&StL took control of Des Moines and Fort Dodge in 1905, it gained operating rights over Milwaukee Road's I&D Division from Ruthven to Spencer, thirteen miles, in the process linking its otherwise disconnected routes and creating through operation from Des Moines and Fort Dodge as well as northward to Minneapolis and southward to Storm Lake, until the latter route was abandoned south of Spencer in 1936. In 1948, M&StL offered a daily-except-Sunday passenger turn from Fort Dodge to Estherville, serving Spencer, in addition to tri-weekly freight operation.

By 1948, the era of steam at Spencer had passed on M&StL in favor of RS-1 diesels from Alco, and in June, M&StL discontinued passenger service that for years had been provided by self-contained gas–electric cars. Pacifics drew Milwaukee Road's *Sioux,* and Mikados held down most I&D freight movements, but two-unit EMDs (Electro-Motive Division) handled flagship time freights 62 and 63, the former a "meat train" expediting eastbound packing house products from Spencer and other on-line points. Prairies and later Consolidations and Mikados handled switching duties as the "Spencer Patrol." On the Iowa Division, heavier demand during the summer tourist season brought out high-drivered but elderly Atlantics for the passenger trains, gas–electric otherwise, with Consolidations assigned to all freights. Over time – actually, over a very short period of time – the scene changed dramatically. Diesels replaced steam, and the Des Moines passenger came off. In 1960, the *Sioux* made its final runs, and M&StL disappeared into the bowels of C&NW. Declines in train frequency presaged wholesale line abandonments and change of ownership on what remained.

Diesel power for the *Sioux* varied by manufacturer: Fairbanks Morse; Electro-Motive Division of General Motors; and every so often Alco's token, "Old Maud," 14-A and 14-B. This is the view from the fireman's seat of 18-B, an EMD product, looking west through Milwaukee Road's yard. Reefers on the right are for Spencer Packing. Spring 1950.

Milwaukee's famous *Olympian Hiawatha* in Spencer? Not hardly.
But Fairbanks Morse giants in pairs typically assigned to that
transcontinental train also showed up on trains 11 and 22, the
Sioux. Water was put on both units at Spencer to supply steam
boilers necessary for heat and air-conditioning. July 1951.

Milwaukee Road in the summer of 1948 assigned elderly but high-stepping B-4 Atlantic 4–4–2s on the Des Moines–Spirit Lake passenger run. They finished out their few remaining days strutting, ungainly, through Iowa cornfields with jobs out of Des Moines to Madrid and Spirit Lake. Traffic volumes on the I&D and Iowa divisions at Spencer were adequate to demand a significant water treatment plant along with large twin tanks. Train 33, August 1948.

CMStP&P in the late 1940s and into the next decade handled midway-show personnel and equipage for Spencer's famous Clay County Fair. In 1948, for example, it brought in and later took out Hennies Brothers Shows – "The World's Largest and Newest Midway" and "40 double-length railroad cars of fun." Other troupes and their impedimenta arrived in baggage cars hooked to the rear of train 33 up from Des Moines. Such was the case in September 1951 when 2–8–0 1287 was recruited from its normal freight duties to handle an enlarged train 33. Perhaps this special movement was on behalf of Sally Rand, the internationally known fan dancer who was sometimes an attraction at the fair.

Gas–electric cars on the Des Moines–Spirit Lake passenger trains had been the norm since 1936, except during the summer tourist season when steam reappeared to handle longer trains to and from the Iowa Great Lakes. The arrival at Spencer from Des Moines was at the late noon hour, a schedule usually met despite twenty-two station stops en route. Train 33 is about to pass through the spring switch and on to the I&D main over the M&StL crossing four blocks east of the passenger station. May 1951.

35

Train 33 brought a predictably heavy volume of mail and express up from Des Moines. To the left is the locomotive that soon will take Iowa Division way-freight 62 on its rounds to Perry. On the right beyond the near platform and the I&D main is Milwaukee Road's substantial wood-frame passenger depot and the Railway Express Agency office. April 1951.

Some days are better than others. A nearly one-hour-late train 33 in charge of gas-electric car 5932 had bucked snow nearly all the way from Des Moines on this February day in 1951 when public schools at Spencer had been called off because of foul weather. A few minutes after leaving Spencer to complete the run northward to Spirit Lake, the train got stuck on a slight grade in a snow-filled cut south of Fostoria. It extracted itself, backed gingerly to Spencer and around the west leg of the wye, and tied up in front of the depot – defeated. A C-5 Consolidation 2–8–0 taken from the Spencer Patrol would head the train back to Des Moines at 7:02 PM.

Milwaukee Road's elementary engine facility at Spencer was up the Spirit Lake line at West Tenth Street, a couple of dismounted boxcars serving as office and storage for supplies and three unsheltered stub tracks for locomotives. To the north, on the west side of the track, was the coal dock, a spur to take gondolas loaded with company fuel, a platform for perhaps sixteen 500-pound cast steel buckets into which coal was scooped by hand, and an air-activated derrick that engine crews used to lift loaded buckets and swing them over the tender for dumping. It was, to say the least, unsophisticated and labor intensive.

A long-standing tradition on the Spirit Lake branch, technically part of the I&D Division, although Iowa Division crews worked through from Des Moines and Perry, was ice harvesting in winter months at Okoboji (from East Lake Okoboji). Ice harvesting required a daily turn from Spencer with empty boxcars up and return with loads destined for CMStP&P icing facilities at Mason City and elsewhere. Ten-wheeler 1019, class G-8, done for the day, is tied up at the Spencer engine facility. January 1953.

Tom Sawyer had nothing on Roy Hannah, Milwaukee Road's engine watchman and the man who shoveled coal into 500-pound buckets at the fuel doc. Hannah was perfectly willing to allow young rail enthusiasts the privilege of scooping ash from cinder pads at the engine facility after he had knocked the fire from locomotives in his care. As a reward, the youngsters then could take the fireman's seat box and dream the dream of life on the rails. Such a vantage point also allowed a fine view of the "gas car" bringing train 36 in from Spirit Lake en route to Des Moines. May 1951.

The engineer on I&D 64 this overcast day in August 1951 seems intent on getting a wheel on his train as soon as possible, and he will do so as soon as the M&StL crossing is cleared. Counterpart train 65 came and went in darkness. On clear, calm nights one could hear its authoritative whistle from as far away as Dickens, seven miles east, and again every ninety seconds or so as its L2 raced tonnage toward Spencer, shutting off before the city limits and getting speed down to fifteen miles per hour over the M&StL crossing.

The death knell sounded for Milwaukee Road's Des Moines–Spirit Lake passenger operation in June 1951 when the Post Office Department failed to renew the vital mail contract. The trains limped on for several months, however, and the always-generous William D. "Gas-car Bill" Chase, engineer on 33–36, was happy to have company in the cab. Indeed, if central casting had been asked to supply a locomotive engineer, Chase would have appeared. Big, bluff, garrulous, and an innovative and accomplished curser, Chase was a railroader's railroader. He also was an accomplished amateur golfer, an extremely unusual trait for members of the operating crafts at that time. Chase's work assignment at CMStP&P was to take passenger trains three times weekly from Des Moines to Spirit Lake and return. It gave him four days off, plenty of opportunity in season to hone his golfing talents. April 5, 1952.

Barely a mile east of town, Mikado
500 has I&D train 64 up to forty
miles per hour. September 1952.

Snow – the perennial natural enemy of railroading in northwest Iowa. A blizzard in February
1953 brought out Work Extra 435 to clear the I&D
line east from Spencer, but there was at that
time no substitute for the local section gang's
manual labor in cleaning up the station platform.

By August 1953, steam's only regular assignments on the I&D between Mason City and
Sanborn, through Spencer, were trains 64 and
65 and the Spencer Patrol. L2b 466 has the
main track with a hefty 64 this day. Mail for
the eastbound *Sioux* this evening is already on
the platform. At left is Milwaukee's utilitarian
freight depot; at right is the road's substantial
water treatment facility that will serve no
purpose in the age of full dieselization.

Milwaukee Road once stabled a substantial roster of Prairies, but by 1948 their numbers were dwindling. Capable of handling road assignments or switching chores, these 2–6–2s frequently were found on the Spencer Patrol in the late 1940s. April 1948.

The illusion of urgency. A slow shutter speed gives the impression that C5 1275 is rushing into Spencer with the Spirit Lake–Perry way freight. In fact, maximum authorized speed for freights was thirty miles per hour. Summer 1951.

Steam disappeared from this part of the Iowa Division on Saturday, February 28, 1953, with C5 1275 having the dubious honor. Train 62 between Gillett Grove and Webb.

Facing:

Milwaukee Road innovated with new diesel power on the Iowa Division, sending two six-axle SD7s up on train 63 from Perry and turning them on a tight meet at Spencer to return on 62, using the dinky center cab switcher 1709 on the Spencer–Spirit Lake leg. It was a failed practice; 1709 was not up to the task. 2210 and sister have just arrived from Perry. 1709 is at center, with Spencer Patrol's L2b 494 at right. April 1953.

Chunky Consolidation 1265 has brought Iowa Division way freight 63 up from Perry, and the fireman has topped off the tank (see the condensation line on the tender). Soon the train will cross Grand Avenue and turn up the east leg of the wye for Spirit Lake, likely arriving there on time at 3:45 PM. C5s were rated at 2,700 tons on the line through Spencer.

For a period in 1953, the Spencer Patrol was called and tied up at Sanborn, thirty miles to the west. Would I like to ride over to Sanborn one evening? Does a bear like honey? Amen. Engineer Charles Lusk and his clothing always appeared at war with soap and water, but he was generous and obliging. Extra 1209 West about to leave Spencer with a short drag (three loads, five empties, 475 tons) and work to do at intervening stations Everly and Hartley. July 1953.

Milwaukee Road cooperated with Spencer's radio station KICD and the local chamber of commerce to deliver Santa Claus annually for a pre-Christmas visit to the depot at Spencer. December 1953.

The era of regularly scheduled steam-powered trains at Spencer ended on February 16, 1954, when L2b 444 shepherded way freight 64 from Sanborn to Mason City. A few months later, G8 4–6–0 1004 pushed a weed sprayer through town and in the summer of 1955 G7 4–6–0 1083 performed similarly indelicate duties. Steam would come no more.

In the spring of 1954, Milwaukee Road briefly assigned Fairbanks Morse H-16-66 1,600 hp units on Perry–Spencer–Spirit Lake freights. On April 20, 1954, Extra 2116 handled heavy tonnage on a southbound run just east of Spencer.

When Milwaukee Road discontinued its Des Moines–Spirit Lake passenger service after April 12, 1952, its *Sioux*, trains 11 and 22, to and from Chicago on the east and Canton, South Dakota, on the west, offered Spencer its sole passenger offering. Train 11 at the east edge of town arriving from Chicago. The track in the foreground is that of the Iowa Division to and from Perry and Des Moines. August 1955.

During the last half of the 1950s, Milwaukee Road's Monday-through-Friday switch job at Mason City cut off four of the *Sioux*'s normal seven cars, including the sleeper, which left only a bobtailed train to the west. No. 11 between Dickens and Spencer. Summer 1957.

Rank hath its privilege. After CMStP&P removed dining service from its *Sioux* early in the 1950s, a twenty- to twenty-five-minute station stop was permitted at Spencer so that passengers could walk to nearby cafés for a late breakfast or lunch. The conductor went along; the brakeman had to stay with the train. No. 11, August 1956.

Irrespective of the era, there was always work to do when the passenger train arrived. Mail was unloaded from and loaded into the Railway Post Office, and Karl Dickinson, the local agent for Railway Express (in the car), and his driver (on the express cart) could expect some heavy lifting.

Ben Sanders, owner of Spencer's KICD radio, arranged to have a microphone placed on the eaves of Milwaukee Road's passenger depot, and for more than a decade morning personality Mason Dixon made the arrival of no. 11, the westbound *Sioux,* part of his "Yawn Patrol" broadcast, switching on the mike so that listeners could hear the train coming into town. It was a daily ritual at KICD, mixed in with news, weather, and market reports. It also reflected a time when railroad companies and the trains they operated set the tempo of a community. That era passed almost completely during the 1950s, and that passing was reflected at Spencer. Milwaukee Road re-jiggered the schedule for no. 11, making its arrival near noon instead of at the breakfast hour, as had been the case for ages. And, of course, five days a week the train was a mere shadow of its former self. Note the URTX reefers at left being iced before taken to Spencer Packing for loading. No. 11 at the M&StL crossing. July 1957.

Milwaukee Road changed but little the arrival and departure times for train 22, eastbound to Chicago. After the demise of dining service west of Mason City in 1951, Spencer was a "meal stop." Passengers were given twenty-five minutes to walk down Grand Avenue a block or so for a snack or a meal. No. 22, January 2, 1960.

With no switch engine on duty at Mason City, no. 11 on Christmas day 1959 had its full consist (two thirty-foot RPO cars, two storage cars, two coaches, and a sleeper) all the way to Canton, South Dakota, and return as train 22. But no. 11 would not see another Christmas in Iowa. Frank Merchant, Milwaukee Road's hard working and well-respected section foreman at Spencer is at right, likely there to make sure the station platform is clean.

The porter on the last sleeping car out of Spencer (January 3, 1960) was a busy fellow with all berths sold. The *Sioux* would make its final runs west of Madison, Wisconsin, on January 5, 1960.

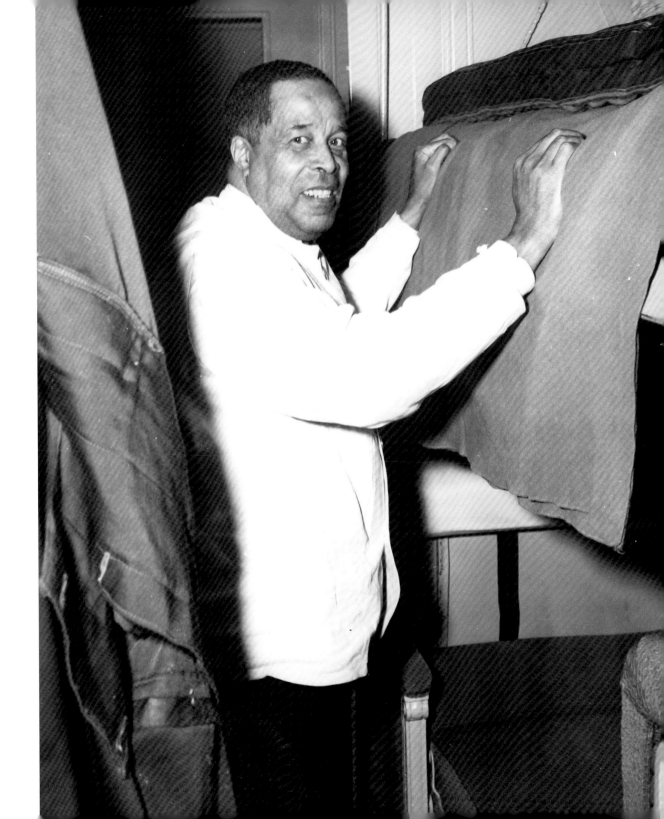

Power assigned to the Spencer Patrol varied greatly over the years. During much of the 1960s, it took the form of a 1,200 hp Baldwin S-12s such as 1925 hurrying eastward from Spencer toward Dickens. Track at left is the Iowa Division. February 1965.

Train 63 still held time-freight status in August 1967, but deteriorating track conditions no longer favored spirited locomotive engineers. Rolling through Dickens, headed for Spencer. August 1967.

In July 1976 there was still meat on the "meat train," but not for long as packers shifted location of their plants away from the upper Midwest and as they increasingly billed product by truck. No. 62 east of Spencer.

Milwaukee Road's dispirited condition is reflected by the ill-kept property in July 1976 *(right and overleaf)*. Train 63.

Hot! Trainmen on this drag up from Perry on the Iowa Division have stripped to the essentials this very warm and humid day in August 1976. Soon they will have their train safely tucked into the yard at Spencer.

When Rock Island sought and obtained permission to abandon parts of its Gowrie–Sibley line, it worked out a deal with CMStP&P for trackage rights from Emmetsburg through Spencer to Hartley, where both Rock Island and Milwaukee Road had access to a large grain shipper. Another part of the arrangement allowed Rock Island over Milwaukee's Iowa Division from Spencer to near Webb, where CRI&P again reached its own rail. On this warm July evening in 1976, a Rock Island train is at Iowa Junction about to head south.

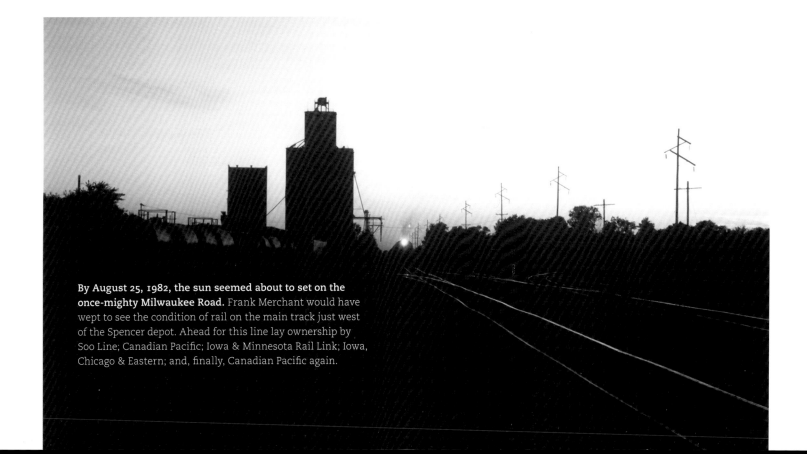

By August 25, 1982, the sun seemed about to set on the once-mighty Milwaukee Road. Frank Merchant would have wept to see the condition of rail on the main track just west of the Spencer depot. Ahead for this line lay ownership by Soo Line; Canadian Pacific; Iowa & Minnesota Rail Link; Iowa, Chicago & Eastern; and, finally, Canadian Pacific again.

Gone by the summer of 1980 were trains 62 and 63. Milwaukee Road instead offered customers a more random schedule. The Rail Detector cars at right had their work cut out. Eastbound.

There were a few passengers and a bit of express for M&StL's train 18 on this Saturday in April 1948. Jake Fritz, the company's cashier at Spencer, hands up company mail to the baggage man. RPO service had ended a few months earlier, and the train's final runs would come on Thursday, June 24, 1948.

M&StL in 1948 and 1949 offered tri-weekly freight service with train 57 arriving in Spencer on Mondays, Wednesdays, and Fridays with tonnage from Fort Dodge. Another crew went on duty at Spencer on 57's arrival, did the local switching and continued onward to Estherville, doing the switching there, exchanging cars with train 60 from Winthrop, Minnesota, making up tomorrow's train 61, and returning to Spencer with service to Raileigh, Terril, and Langdon en route and performing any remaining switching at Spencer and making up 56's train before tying up. The return by 56 was on Tuesdays, Thursdays, and Saturdays. On this crisp spring day in 1950 Alco 948 is backing train 56 to the CMStP&P interlocker and will soon head east to Ruthven, thirteen miles, by trackage rights over Milwaukee Road.

By 1951, M&StL operations were modified so that trains 57 and 56 operated all the way from Fort Dodge to Estherville and return. Sixteen-hour days were routine. No. 57, a mile above Spencer. June 1951.

M&StL's conventional practice in dealing with snow, a perennial problem, especially north of Spencer between Terril and Estherville, was to call a work extra from Fort Dodge with a Russell plow to clear the line and widen the cuts. The crew of Extra 746 has opened the line and now points the train back to Fort Dodge – but won't leave until they get some "beans" at Spencer.

It would be a long night before Work Extra 1044 and Russell plow X-1003 opened the snow-clogged line between Spencer and Estherville. Leaving Spencer against a setting sun, February 1952.

M&StL linked its "B-Line" (Winthrop–Spencer) with its "C-Line" (Tara–Ruthven) by trackage rights between Spencer and Ruthven. M&StL locomotive engineers enjoyed the opportunity to travel forty-nine miles per hour on that thirteen-mile stretch. Milwaukee Road dispatchers often annulled 56 and ran it extra, as was the case on this Saturday in September 1952. Two miles east of Spencer. The track in the foreground is Milwaukee Road's Iowa Division.

M&StL crewmen were generous and accommodating.
Engineer James W. Murphy, seniority date 7–18–1910, and
Conductor Charles A. Brown, seniority date 8–5–1912.

Business on M&StL at Spencer late in December and into the new year was slack, with number 57 on December 29, 1952, reflecting as much. Beryl H. Wiles, the regularly assigned "hind-end" brakeman (on the caboose platform), and relief conductor Max A. Sedelmeir, who will board the caboose as it comes by, were longtime employees. At right behind the caboose is the Country Club Beer warehouse, Conductor Charles Brown's favorite customer. The open ground at left had been the site of M&StL's well and water tank in steam days as well as the first depot, only recently replaced by a steel structure.

Cupalo caboose 1119 was Conductor's Brown's home away from home and his well-appointed office, too.

Brakeman Lyle Severson soon will get the switch at Milwaukee Junction so Engineer James Murphy can head train 56 onto Milwaukee Road trackage for the sprint to Ruthven. To the left are signals governing the M&StL–Milwaukee crossing, and beyond on a Milwaukee spur are URTX's refrigerator cars being iced for the movement of meat coming from Spencer Packing. Summer 1954.

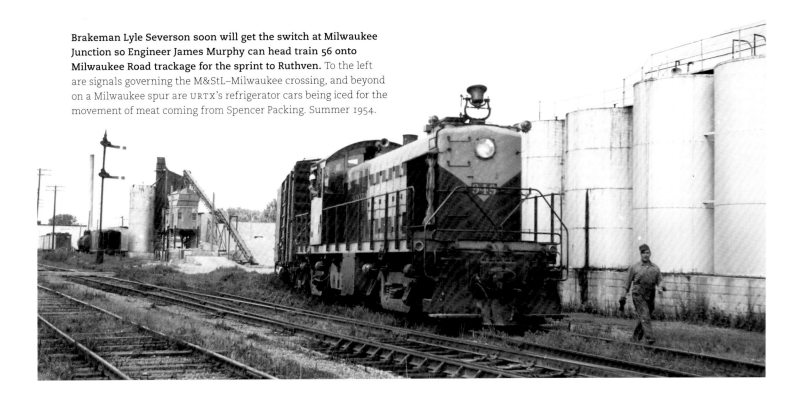

On May 20, 1953, M&StL hosted the Des Moines Goodwill (chamber of commerce) train from Estherville to Spencer. Alco 446 and heater car 501 caught the assignment of wheeling six heavyweight sleepers and their ebullient ambassadors. It must have been an entertaining ride overnight from Estherville on M&StL's uncertain track.

Engineer James Murphy has 56's extra at
track speed on CMStP&P near Lost Island
Lake east of Dickens. February 13, 1954.

M&StL's resourceful shopmen at Cedar Lake (Minneapolis) managed to successfully and inexpensively prepare some of the road's extensive Alco fleet for multiple-unit operation. Enginemen loved to "open them up" on Milwaukee Road trackage. Eastbound between Spencer and Dickens, September 1956.

GE-25 was rebuilt into a company weed sprayer in June 1957. Two years later, it found much to do five miles north of Spencer near Langdon.

Train 56 rolls into Spencer from the north. Late October 1960.

October 31, 1960 – a day to remember or a day to forget. Conductor Max A. Sedelmeier (*lower right*); Fireman Demar C. Blankenhagen (*walkway*); and Engineer Paul K. Brubaker, (*cab*), would be Chicago & North Western employees the following day, M&StL having perished at midnight.

Appearances were deceiving. Alcos were gone, but replacement EMD GP-9s still wore M&StL numbers and paint and trailed M&StL cabooses. But the old road was gone. A C&NW train is in this sunset view a mile north of Spencer in August 1961.

Grain moving in boxcars had been the lifeblood for M&StL, and it continued so for C&NW. Trains now moved as extras on irregular schedules, e.g., Extra 604 in the stark spring of 1962, just north of Spencer.

Gone was the M&StL sign from the Spencer depot, gone were M&StL colors, greatly reduced was maintenance of way (notice the weeds), and on site was a dog's breakfast of motive power and equipment.

Though C&NW had abandoned the line between Terril and Estherville in its well-known style of chopping off the dog's tail an inch at a time, the illusion of a healthy traffic base on the stub north to Langdon and Terril was created in the early 1970s when, instead of setting out Spencer tonnage from Fort Dodge, crews took the entire train north and then doubled it back after setting out or picking up local cars. Northbound near Langdon, summer 1972.

Walter J. O'Connor, like most engineers on the former M&StL out of Fort Dodge, was astonished to have cab units in local service – nice in roadwork, not so nice in switching. Summer, 1972, en route from Spencer to Terril.

The southbound trainload of corncobs will pause briefly at Spencer's Tenth Avenue East grade crossing so that Brakeman Don Messerly can hand a very young Knute L. Hofsommer to his father after a ride on the locomotive from Langdon, adequately affirming a long family tradition. August 21, 1980.

Birds have been startled by the rumbling of Extra 4448 West between Dickens and Spencer on July 29, 1981.
The empty gondolas will be loaded with scrap by Shine Brothers, a longtime M&StL and then C&NW customer.

Picking up several boxcars loaded with low revenue corncobs at Terril and then rolling slowly back to Spencer over bridge 194. July 29, 1981.

Brakeman Billy Fallon, in a time-honored tradition, opens the gate over the Milwaukee Road crossing to allow Extra 4518 East into the Spencer Yard.

Meredith Johnston, left, and Vernie G. Hofsommer, right, make photographic record of the Spencer agent and the crew of the last C&NW train out of town on August 11, 1981.

Two venerable institutions in demise, the M&StL (now C&NW) and the neighborhood grocery store. The railroad on August 11, 1981, would predecease the store.

Diverse. That is the appropriate word to describe Iowa's railroad experience. The state was dense with vital horizontal lines from east to west that were overlaid by equally vital vertical lines from north to south. It was honeycombed with branches and the site of several impressive electric roads, and Iowa was even home for a smattering of short-line companies. On these rails passed humble locals in freight and passenger service, "Red Ball" time freights, and a host of elegant streamliners, *Chiefs, Rockets, Cities, Zephyrs,* and *Hiawathas* among them. From a railroad perspective, it was a land of infinite variety. But the focus here is "off the main lines."

Light Pacific 1001 caught the assignment for local freight duty on Illinois Central's Cherokee–Sioux Falls line this bright June day in 1951. Train 792, seen here at Sheldon, like its counterpart 791, was mixed – carrying passengers, if any, in the caboose.

Pacifics were standard motive power on many Milwaukee Road passenger trains across the company's network in Iowa. On one blustery day in November 1951, 4–6–2 820 waits patiently at Sioux City for a mid-afternoon departure to Yankton, Mitchell, and Aberdeen with train 123.

Being a brakeman on a passenger run was not always what it was cracked up to be. Part of the job description for the Milwaukee Road Des Moines–Spirit Lake run was to turn the gas–electric car on the "Armstrong" turntable at Spirit Lake. William Moody has shed his snappy passenger uniform in favor of denim for this duty on April 5, 1952.

Ray Saugling, CMStP&P's agent at Ruthven, in a time-honored tradition has his train-order fork ready for the hind end of time-freight 63. November 1951.

Rock Island took delivery of this 380 hp Davenport–Bessler yard goat in 1940. Twelve years later, it awaited duty at Estherville, having relieved a 200-class 0–6–0 that had worked there in the era of steam.

In May 1951, C&NW operated three daily passenger trains in each direction between the Twin Cities and Omaha. The daylight offerings, trains 203 and 204, the *North American*, boasted a consist of head-end cars, coaches, a café parlor car, and a Los Angeles sleeper via Union Pacific at Omaha. Train 204 made a brief stop at Sheldon each day at 1:26 PM.

Milwaukee's brawny L3 344 heads a heavy northbound freight out of Marquette along the Mississippi River on May 31, 1953. CMStP&P's protocols often called for an extra caboose behind the locomotive to accommodate the needs of the head brakeman.

Iowa was well seasoned with electric railways. Cedar Rapids & Iowa City, one of these, linking the two cities of its corporate name, in 1938 had advertised eleven daily passenger turns, but traffic volumes rapidly eroded after World War II. On May 30, 1953, the road ended all passenger service. Car 120 is about to leave Iowa City for the last time.

A nasty head-on collision of an eight-car C&NW (Omaha Road) passenger train and a snowplow extra north of Hospers required services of two wrecking crews to pick up the mess. February 22, 1953.

Wayside depots were ubiquitous across the expanse of Iowa during the early 1950s. C&NW's facility at Linn Grove, in the northwest portion of the state, was typical. May 1952.

On Sunday, July 26, 1953, Fort Dodge, Des Moines & Southern ran an excursion covering all of its lines north of Boone. At the Lehigh stop, Vernie G. Hofsommer has the catbird seat.

Waterloo, Cedar Falls & Northern (WCF&N) was a muscular road with a good base of freight traffic, but continued electrical operation was doomed when a devastating fire at the Waterloo shops took most of its equipment. That bad news was in the future when this view was made on October 13, 1953.

WCF&N was justifiably proud of its passenger equipment and service. Here, car 100 with train 15 from Cedar Rapids to Waterloo is about to duck under Milwaukee Road's Chicago–Council Bluffs main west of Marion on February 7, 1954. Track at left is IC's Manchester–Cedar Rapids branch.

Tiny Mason City & Clear Lake was happy to show off its equipment at Emery on March 27, 1954.

Wabash certainly spent no money advertising its wonderful anachronism – daily mixed-train service into Keokuk from Bluffs, Illinois, powered by ancient Mogul 2–6–0s. Long shadows demonstrate that train 12 is well off its scheduled departure time of 1:30 PM. Keokuk, September 7, 1953.

September 11, 1955. A somber day. Ever-gracious Fort Dodge, Des Moines & Southern staged a final farewell to the big yellow cars on an abbreviated excursion from Boone. Trolley wire came down shortly thereafter. Near Ericson, southeast of Boone.

Milwaukee Road train 24, Cedar Rapids–Calmar service, churns out of Fayette Cut on November 7, 1953.

L2b 466 blasts into Calmar with Milwaukee Road's Mason City–Marquette time-freight 68. November 7, 1953.

Milwaukee Road roundhouse personnel and enginemen strike a convivial pose at Cedar Rapids on November 7, 1953.

Rock Island's 1250, wearing a resplendent paint scheme, hurries a westbound freight near Rossie in an archetypical example of branch-line railroading in Iowa during the early 1950s. March 1954.

Why would anybody be taking our picture seems the question for both the fireman of Milwaukee Road's time freight 63 and the telegraph operator at Emmetsburg. Note the train-order fork with orders or messages for the hind end to the right of the operator. May 1954.

The era of branch-line passenger service quickly wound down during the 1950s. The Post Office Department hastened this pattern when it ruled that postal clerks would no longer be allowed to work in Railway Post Office apartments on gas–electric cars. Carriers were confronted with the need to acquire new equipment, re-engine old cars with diesel prime movers, or seek discontinuance of trains to which gas–electric units were assigned. For its part, Milwaukee Road declined to invest in what it considered to be terminally ailing branch-line runs. The end came for trains 23 and 24 on August 10, 1954, along Milwaukee's 134-mile route that wandered around much of northeastern Iowa to connect Cedar Rapids with Calmar. Train 24 left Cedar Rapids at 5:30 AM, joined CMStP&P's Chicago–Council Bluffs main and proceeded through Marion to Paralta, nine miles, then diverged through Anamosa, Monticello, and Strawberry Point to intercept Milwaukee Road's cross-state Iowa & Dakota Division at Jackson Junction, and eastward eleven miles to gain Calmar at 11:05 AM. Engineer Walter E. Hollenbeck gives a friendly wave from the cab of 5937, train 24, as it passes through Fort Atkinson for the final time.

Accommodations could be made. It was, after all, the last trip for train 23. Engineer Hollenbeck stopped the train in Fayette Cut so this image could be made.

C&NW agreed to tack on passenger cars at the rear of regularly scheduled train 55 for those wishing to ride from Eagle Grove to Elmore, Minnesota, and return. It proved a dreary, rainy day, but doubleheaded Rls 1329 and 159 put on a spectacular show wheeling the heavy train. Nearing Bancroft, April 23, 1955.

Chicago & North Western agreed to run an excursion from Webster City through Jewell and Gifford to Alden on Sunday, June 27, 1954. It proved a splendid outing, a chamber of commerce day, gawkers flocking to every station to see the steam-powered train, recalling an earlier era – the steam-car civilization. Nearing Alden.

The time of steam was rapidly coming to an end, but on June 19, 1955, C&NW again consented to a special excursion to Alden, this time from Tama. There would be no repeat performances.

The westbound *Sioux* rolls into Charles City promptly at 7:22 AM on June 5, 1955, with an unusually long consist behind 14-B (Alco DL-109 re-engined with EMD prime mover) and two supporting Fairbanks Morse units. It was 328 miles from its Chicago origin, 206 miles from its Canton, South Dakota, destination.

On January 1, 1958, C&NW acquired the assets of Litchfield & Madison (L&M), a short but important bridge line giving C&NW access to the St. Louis market. By the following summer, L&M power mixed with that of C&NW at Belle Plaine.

Chicago Great Western's Minneapolis–Kansas City passenger offering by the late 1950s was pedestrian at best, taking more than sixteen hours to make the 542-mile run, but the trains did supply passenger opportunity as well as important mail and express needs for fifty communities en route. Train 6, north of Hudson, March 1959.

The mail messenger at Grand Junction has exchanged pouches with the RPO clerk, and soon the engineer on M&StL's GE-28 will open the throttle and take train 2 over C&NW's double-diamonds and on toward the Des Moines destination. July 1951.

In 1945, M&StL acquired two three-unit FT sets from EMD to power its flagship trains 19 and 20 on daily 476-mile sprints between Minneapolis and Peoria. Additional reserve power came later. On March 28, 1953, 445 takes a breather at Marshalltown.

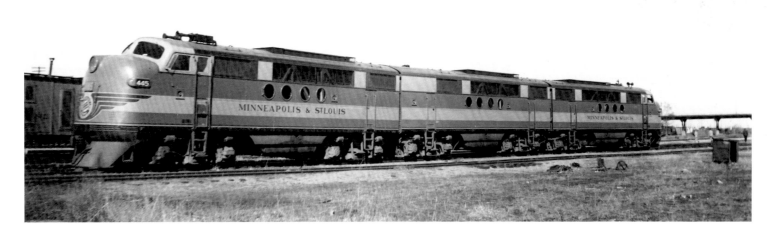

There was much about Minneapolis & St. Louis after a bitter proxy fight in 1954 that was the same and much that was different. The route structure was unchanged, but a new, aggressive management team quickly put its stamp on the property. Change in corporate colors and locomotive numbering were tiny reflections of the new order.

Its station stop at Britt completed, M&StL train 1 hurries northward toward its eventual Minneapolis destination. March 27, 1954.

M&StL's train 7 made its daily departure from Albia in the wee hours of the morning, having connected there with Wabash's St. Louis–Des Moines train and also having received passengers, mail, and express from trains of the Burlington Route. By 9:55 A M, it was rushing toward the Chicago Great Western crossing at Manly. After a brief station stop in that community and even briefer stops at Kensett, Northwood, and Glenville, it would breeze into Albert Lea, Minnesota, at 10:45. July 1954.

Train 19, masquerading as Extra 147, barrels into Hampton on its daily sojourn from Bartlett Yard (Peoria) to Cedar Lake (Minneapolis), covering the intervening distance in about seventeen hours. M&StL's locomotive 147 was the only example of an EMD F2 on the company roster. It joined FTs 445 and 545 in protecting trains 19 and 20. August 15, 1954.

On a pleasant spring morning in 1960, train 20, pride of the fleet, bangs over the C&NW crossing at Gifford with three F units and a recently acquired GP-9.

Alcos in full throat – locomotives 225 and 207 (formerly 1049 and 845) lift a heavy train of grain and rock away from the "'pit" southward toward Gilmore City. September 5, 1959.

The peace of a spring afternoon in 1960
at Faulkner is shattered as M&StL's
time-freight 19 roars northward.

Time-freight 20 eases through Oskaloosa on a warm August day in 1960. Behind is Minneapolis, 289 miles; ahead is Peoria, 187 miles.

Late in 1958, M&StL acquired 14 GP-9 locomotives from EMD and placed them in service around the system. One of them, 709, takes train 50 through a snow squall south of Badger. The Fort Dodge terminal is only a few miles distant. Train 50 typically did the local work between Albert Lea and Fort Dodge. Its counterpart, train 51, handled perishables and other time-sensitive freight, much of it handed off by IC following interchange with UP at Council Bluffs, on an expedited schedule to make connection for Minneapolis and St. Paul at Albert Lea.

**M&StL and IC joined in
an innovative way to
expedite lading between
Minneapolis and Chicago
via Albert Lea and
Waterloo, sharing in
equal portions locomo-
tives and cabooses.** IC's
train AC-2 hustles toward
Waterloo near Janesville.
Two cars of meat from
Wilson & Company's
Albert Lea plant have
been added behind the
second unit. April 1960.

**Mason City was served
by Milwaukee Road,
M&StL, C&NW, CGW,
and Mason City & Clear
Lake, and it was a
crew-change point and
important service facility
for CMStP&P Road and
C&NW.** In addition to its
vital I&D Division across
northern Iowa, Milwaukee
also had a line linking
Mason City and Austin,
Minnesota. Northbound,
February 1960.

CGW train 192 hurries through Lanesboro on September 23, 1965, with a long consist of mixed freight including livestock and packing-house products from South Omaha on the point.

Chicago Great Western's trains 5 and 6, in Twin Cities–Kansas City service, lived on borrowed time. Green Mountain in 1910 was the scene of Iowa's worst railroad tragedy, but there were no problems on this cold day in March 1961 when no. 6 bored through town. The end came for regularly scheduled passenger trains at Oelwein – Chicago Great Western's hub and headquarters city, on April 28, 1962, when train 6 made its final call.

C&NW continued to offer daily-except-Sunday freight service on the former M&StL between Albert Lea and Fort Dodge. There was no work for no. 50 at Badger on this mild January day, January 1961.

Bright but bitterly cold. Train 50 has left Emmons, on the Iowa–Minnesota border, with a long train of mixed freight and empty boxcars. There would be an abundance of local work along the line before reaching the Fort Dodge terminal.

Britt always was a "good station," i.e., it produced considerable revenue. No. 50 this spring morning in 1962 would be much at work with local switching before heading its heavy train southward.

Fairfield was home during the early 1960s. It was served by Chicago Burlington & Quincy's main line across southern Iowa from Chicago to Council Bluffs, and Chicago, Rock Island & Pacific, whose Golden State route crossed CB&Q at that location. Rock Island's venerable tower was a busy place. CB&Q at the time scheduled a dozen passenger trains daily and perhaps a matching dozen freights like this one headed westbound.

The tower was the place to observe railroading at Fairfield, and Rock Island's Jim Harris, second-trick operator, was always welcoming.

Great excitement always occasioned when Burlington Route operated steam-powered excursions. Its famous 4–8–4 5632 pounds westbound over the Rock Island diamond in June 1963 with an elegant assortment of equipment to delight its lucky patrons.

During the age of railways, depots were one of the few places in a community where lights burned all night, forcefully proclaiming that railroads were at the heart of American life. Nightime lights still burned in depots at some Iowa locations, but railroads no longer held center stage. The erosion would continue as railroads got out of the less-than-carload freight business and as passenger trains with attendant mail and express business disappeared. Fairfield, June 1970.

By 1963, this senior engineman on CB&Q's Fort Madison–Stockport nightly turn reflected the dress of the "modern railroader." He was wistful about the passing of steam but had no desire to turn back the pages of time. December 6, 1963.

Illinois Central's *Hawkeye* provided no-nonsense overnight service from Chicago to **Sioux City.** It was right on "the advertised" in its early morning arrival at Storm Lake this balmy summer morning in 1966.

Headed for home. With the sun at its back, this CB&Q local bound for Burlington stirs little dust as it rattles down what at one time had been narrow-gauge track between Winfield and Mount Union. June 1963.

THE NORTH AMERICAN RAILROAD INDUSTRY WENT
through monumental change during the 1950s – conversion
from steam to diesel motive power, discontinuance of branch-
line passenger service, closing of rural stations, decline of
electric-traction roads, and even shrinkage of plant. Iowa and
neighboring states were a microcosm of the entire package.

Great Northern's (GN) motive-power assignments in August 1951 at Sioux Falls, South
Dakota, were representative of change occurring
throughout the industry. Newly arrived diesel
road switchers such as 636, from Electro-Motive
Division of General Motors, handled freight
duties (a daily-except-Sunday turn to Garretson,
a yard job, and calls as needed to Yankton). The
venerable 2–8–0 at left stands ready as relief,
but calls were few. GN predecessor Willmar &
Sioux Falls had completed a line linking those
two communities in 1881. GN itself put down
the fifty-eight-mile route to Yankton in 1893.

Atchison, Topeka & Santa Fe Prairie-type locomotives were intercepted in branch-line service near Holly, Colorado, and at Jetmore, Kansas, on July 19, 1952.

Steam also held sway at Great Northern's Kelly Lake Yard, where 0–8–0 822 stayed busy throughout the shipping season shunting and sorting iron ore from an assortment of Mesabi Range pits – ore destined for GN's huge loading docks on Lake Superior at Allouez, Wisconsin. August 6, 1953.

Northern Pacific in and about Duluth, Minnesota, in 1953 remained a bastion of steam, with mostly 0–6–0s, 2–6–2s, and 2–8–2s. The Duluth engine terminal and local switching assignments reflected as much. August 2, 1953.

Duluth, Missabe & Iron Range (DM&IR) thrust its broad shoulders across Minnesota's vast Vermillion and Mesabi iron ranges. This included a 118-mile route from Duluth through Two Harbors to Ely and Winton, where DM&IR provided passenger service with an RDC3 – "elements of stainless steel and internal combustion," as writer David P. Morgan put it. Ely, August 3, 1953.

Proud little Chicago & Illinois Midland showed off its Springfield engine facility for attendees of the National Railway Historical Society's annual meeting in **1953.** And while it previously had discontinued passenger operations, management kept trim 4–4–0s available for admiration of visitors. September 6, 1953.

Litchfield & Madison (L&M), "The St. Louis Gateway Route," provided daily coordinated freight service in a way that gave Chicago & North Western access to the vital East St. Louis Gateway. On September 7, 1953, a brace of shiny, 1,600 hp L&M Alco RS-3s whisked tonnage southward at Edwardsville, Illinois.

As was the case for most railroads at the time, Wabash was in a race to announce its complete dieselization. Not surprisingly, then, it did nothing to advertise its steam holdout – indeed, its Mogul anomaly – at Bluffs, Illinois. Weight restrictions on the Illinois River bridge at Meredosia, Illinois, prevented Wabash from operating anything heavier than ancient F-4 Moguls on its line up from Bluffs to Keokuk, Iowa. Trains 3 and 12 in the *Official Guide* were shown as "Freight." So, too, were they shown as "Local Freight" in the company's Decatur Division employee timetables, but with this note: "Nos. 3 and 12 carry passengers." Indeed, they were mixed trains. On the bright Sunday morning of October 18, 1953, Moguls 576 and 587 were allowed to slumber in the Bluffs engine house. No such luck for sister 573, which drew the Keokuk turn that day.

Wabash F-4s were restricted to trains of a mere 710 tons between Bluffs and Clayton (thirty-two miles), although they could manage 1,740 tons from Clayton to Keokuk (forty-three miles), but only if the temperature was above thirty degrees and there was "not much wind." And they were "hand bombers" – i.e., every piece of coal had to be shoveled into the hungry firebox by Mike Seeman, the hardworking fireman. Hand-firing a steam locomotive was as much an art as it was hard work. Air-operated firebox doors opened quickly by stepping on a foot pedal and closed just as quickly when pressure came off the pedal. It seemed simple enough, but it was not at all simple, especially at speed or on rough track. The fireman typically put his back against the side of the cab for support and then pivoted on his right foot to get a scoop of coal from the tender. The next step required physical dexterity and precise timing. He swung back to propel the scoop of coal to the firebox, hitting the door pedal with his left foot so that the firebox doors opened just before the shovel met the opening. Failure meant a scoopful of coal scattered all over the deck, a judgmental scowl from the engineer, and acute embarrassment. And, oh, yes, the fuel had to be spread evenly across the expanse of the firebox, not merely piled in one spot. October 18, 1953.

Only twenty-three miles separated Bluffs from Mount Sterling, but the demanding grade out of the Illinois River Valley west of Meredosia caused 573's thirsty boiler to convert nearly all of the tender's water supply to steam. And the sweaty fireman looked forward to a break from his valiant labors when the train crawled up to the tank at Mount Sterling. Note the operating timetable in his left hip pocket, a sure and perfect statement as to his authenticity as a railroader.

Mixed trains on the Keokuk Branch were authorized a maximum speed of twenty-five miles per hour, but engineers often winked at the restriction. Drifting westward between Denver and Bentley, Illinois.

A brief stop at Carthage was required to set out some loads and to "take water." Then it was off to Keokuk, 16.2 miles distant. Wabash trains were governed by the rules and timetables of Toledo, Peoria & Western between Elvaston and Hamilton; of the Keokuk Municipal Bridge between Hamilton and Keokuk; and of Chicago, Rock Island & Pacific and Chicago, Burlington & Quincy at Keokuk.

Illinois Central on May 1, 1954, found switching utility for its hardly handsome but certainly effective 0–8–0 3554 at Omaha, Nebraska. But the old soldier had not much longer to serve before replacement by internal combustion.

The small and seemingly sleepy community of Superior, Nebraska, claimed the services of four Class One railroads: Santa Fe, Burlington Route, Missouri Pacific, and North Western. And it featured the rail operation of Ideal Cement, whose employees were dumbfounded when strangers took an interest in their activities on May 27, 1954.

Union Pacific (UP) did not categorically blanket Nebraska, but it clearly lay claim to a major portion of it. In southeastern Nebraska, UP had to share Fairbury, where local 183 toils on May 27, 1954, with rival Rock Island.

San Luis Valley Southern (SLVS) – "Operated for freight service only" – guarded lonely and windswept Blanca, Colorado, where it interchanged its modest business with much larger Denver & Rio Grande Western (D&RGW or Rio Grande). On May 28, 1954, SLVS's ancient 2–8–0 has steam up and will soon begin to putter about.

A three-day excursion on Rio Grande's narrow-gauge network was on its final laps when the train paused at Gato, Colorado, to take water and to allow the engineer time to "oil around." Durango is sixty-one miles to the rear. Chama, New Mexico, is forty-six miles ahead. May 31, 1954.

Chama – a place to take a breather, to change crews, to replenish coal and water for Mikado 487, and to add a helper. Then the spectacular charge toward Cumbres Summit was under way. A local resident and owner of a pickup truck was amazed that a handful of (apparently lunatic) excursionists would hire him and his vehicle to load them up and follow the train, with stops for photographs on demand. Two locomotives coupled were forbidden to cross Lobato Trestle. The train thus stopped, the helper cut off for an independent crossing, the train followed and stopped on yonder side to add the helper, and the noisy and ultimately successful assault up the escarpment to Cumbres was renewed.

Helper and road locomotive alike show clear stacks on their Cumbres trek. The refrigerator car on the drawbar of 2–8–2 487 carried the excursionists' baggage.

D&RGW used 1400s in helper service on the standard-gauge line over La Veta Pass eastward from Alamosa, with C-48 2–8–0s assigned to switching duties as well as road jobs to Antonito and Creede. Standard-gauge steam at Alamosa in the form of venerable 2–8–0s would last into December 1956. Alamosa, June 1, 1954.

Duluth, Winnipeg & Pacific (DW&P) provided access to the head of the lakes for Canadian National. Consolidations like 2458 at the Duluth engine house were typical in freight service. August 16, 1955.

A railroad on stilts. Lengthy and expensive trestlework was required for DW&P to get from its terminal in Duluth to yards and depots of other carriers near Lake Superior. August 16, 1955.

Chicago, Milwaukee, St. Paul & Pacific blanketed much of the Midwest with main lines, secondary routes, and branches. Like other roads in the 1950s, it was at once a study in tradition and change. An elderly but still spritely 4–6–0 1022 shouts her authority at Harmony, Minnesota, on August 9, 1954, as she marches out of town with train 471. Harmony was on Milwaukee Road's Isinours–Caledonia Branch in extreme southeastern Minnesota.

On October 2, 1960, Illinois Central operated a twelve-car excursion in Kentucky from Louisville to Dawson Springs and return. It was headed by elegantly manicured 4–8–2 2613. West of Central City.

Residents of Nortonville, Kentucky, thrill
to see this excursion roar through their
community heading back to Louisville.
They would hear IC's melodic, steamboat-
style whistles no more. October 2, 1960.

132

In 1942, Minneapolis & St. Louis sold its Mogul 66 for scrap, but it ended up with an extended life on Missouri coal hauler Bevier & Southern (B&S). It rested between calls in this autumnal scene at Bevier on September 18, 1960.

Extended life also obtained for CB&Q 2–8–2 4963 as it toiled on for B&S hauling coal up to the CB&Q Route transfer at Bevier from Mine No. Four (14.34 miles). March 24, 1961.

Minneapolis & St. Louis sold all ten of its modern 0–6–0s to run off remaining miles elsewhere. Midland Electric Coal Company acquired six of these, including no. 84 working the four-mile tipple-to-washer line at Middle Grove, Illinois. Stack noise and saucy whistle could give the impression of larger steam locomotives at hard labor. Midland was a good customer for M&StL and then C&NW. April 1963.

Passenger demand was light, but scenery was spectacular for much of Denver & Rio Grande Western's route between Denver and Craig, Colorado. Train 10 awaits its 8:05 departure from Craig on a splendid early October Sunday in 1964. Ahead were 231 miles through Byers Canyon and the Moffat Tunnel to Denver, reached seven hours and fifteen minutes later.

By July 1965, Soo Line's *Winnipeger*, shorn of mail contracts, was down to one head-end car, a coach, and a sleeper (with a diner between Thief River Falls and Winnipeg) and had not long to live. Departing the Milwaukee Road station at Minneapolis for St. Paul, on time at 6:45 AM.

M&StL, the "Home Road" now owned and operated by C&NW, atrophied bit by bit. For a while during the early 1960s, C&NW provided twice-weekly service with one crew all the way from Fort Dodge, Iowa, to Hanska, Minnesota, 159 miles with twenty-four en-route stations. A second caboose provided sleeping quarters for the enginemen. Crews hated the job, calling it the "North to Alaska Run." Grain moving in boxcars remained lifeblood. Northbound between LaSalle and Hanska, Minnesota, November 1961.

As service declined, business declined; as business declined, service declined.
It was never clear which pattern obtained. On this brilliant August day in 1962, however, the lack of demand was fully apparent on the former M&StL line when this northbound local breached the Iowa–Minnesota boundary above Huntington, Iowa, with a single revenue tank in tow.

As late as June 1963, it was impossible to know that C&NW and not M&StL owned the line west from Watertown to Aberdeen and Leola, South Dakota. Alco locomotives and cupola cabooses still wore M&StL livery, but not for long. The line itself was on borrowed time. Heading east, near Bradley.

Doubledheaded 2–8–2s was the norm in wheeling tonnage out of Alamosa and down to Antonito. Empty tanks for Chama are on the point.

THERE IS NO KNOWN ANTIDOTE FOR PERSONS exposed to the Colorado narrow-gauge-railroad virus. Personal infection dated from family trips in 1952 and 1954, categoric affliction came as the result of spending the summer of 1964 at Alamosa, relapse followed the next year, and flare-ups have occurred ever after. Indeed, once fully exposed, there is no cure, no salvation.

The earliest predecessor of Denver & Rio Grande Western, the Denver & Rio Grande (D&RG), was given life by those who saw in it a powerful tool of urban economic imperialism that would make the aspiring city of Denver the commercial center of the whole mountain area and, indeed, the entire Southwest. Begun as a north–south venture hugging the Front Range of the Rocky Mountains, D&RG's promoters contemplated a strategic narrow-gauge route reaching all the way down from Denver to Santa Fe, El Paso, and finally to Mexico City. Three potential routes were studied:

A) Pueblo–Trinidad–Raton Pass
B) Pueblo–Walsenburg–Veta Pass–San Luis Valley
C) Pueblo–Salida–Poncha Pass–San Luis Valley

D&RG did reach Pueblo in 1872, stalled for a variety of reasons, reconsidered its options, and pushed on to Trinidad and La Veta in 1876, focusing now on reaching the San Juan mining country. Rails reached Alamosa on June 26, 1878, then crews pushed south to Antonito, twenty-nine miles, and then west by south, following surveyors who had located a route through the Toltec Gorge District and Conejos Range at Cumbres to tap Chama, New Mexico Territory, late in 1880. The route wound in and out of steep canyons, clung to the sides of sheer cliffs high above foaming streams, and crossed the Colorado–New Mexico boundary a dozen times. The country beyond Chama was rather more hospitable to railroad construction, and D&RG laborers pushed into Durango in 1881, continuing the next season up the Animas River to Silverton. Driving all of it, of course, was the prospect of serving a plethora of mining camps and districts, every one certain to provide D&RG with an abundance of loads and passengers to and from, a sure prescription for prosperity.

Additional D&RG construction turned Alamosa into a railroad hub of considerable note. One line from Alamosa ranged northwestward to Del Norte and South Fork (1881), to Wagon Wheel Gap (1883), and finally to Creede and North

Creede (1891). Another route, springing forth from Villa Grove on D&RG's existing line from Salida over Poncha Pass, pushed down the broad expanse of the San Luis Valley to Alamosa in 1890. This one featured an amazing fifty-three-mile tangent. Even earlier, D&RG fostered a major extension southward from Antonito to Espanola, New Mexico Territory, in 1880 and on to Santa Fe six years later.

In 1888, D&RG operated 1,673 route miles of narrow-gauge railway, but even as it completed these and other narrow-gauge lines, it was standard-gauging main routes. In 1899, D&RG widened its gauge into Alamosa from the east over La Veta Pass. The process continued incrementally up the line to Creede (1902), and a third rail was laid in 1901 between Alamosa and Antonito allowing passage of both narrow- and standard-gauge motive power and equipment. Collectively, this made Alamosa D&RG's "change-of-gauge" point and shop center for many of the company's narrow-gauge locomotives and rolling stock.

In 1905, D&RG put down a standard-gauge line of forty-eight miles from near Durango to Farmington, New Mexico Territory, but in 1923, to reverse the trend, it changed this curious island of standard-gauge operation to narrow gauge.

Change of a corporate nature came in 1920 when Denver & Rio Grande Western (D&RGW or Rio Grande) was incorporated. Its predecessors had struggled financially, and the new company would, too, for several years.

This financial anemia was reflected across D&RGW's narrow-gauge network and, to some extent, was the cause of it. Mines gave out over time, other sources of revenue dried up, and the comparative disadvantage of narrow gauge loomed large. Abandonments followed, including the "Chili" line to Santa Fe in 1941 and the "Valley" line into Alamosa from the north a decade later. By the 1960s, all that remained was Alamosa–Chama–Durango and from Durango, the Farmington and Silverton branches. The future for all of it looked grim.

Nevertheless, in the summer of 1964, business was relatively brisk with trains called two or three times weekly to move pipe and drill mud for the Farmington oil fields and to move machinery and oil from the loading racks at Chama for the refinery at Alamosa, dimension lumber from mills west of Chama, company coal from mines at Monero, a modicum of mixed freight, and, of course, empties in both directions.

Alamosa was Rio Grande's "change-of-gauge" location where trains, both standard gauge and narrow, were broken up or made up. The property was well groomed and the yard often a busy place. D&RGW's depot is at left.

The illusion of high speed. The maximum authorized speed between Alamosa and Antonito was twenty-five miles per hour, a rule breached a bit on occasion. "Dog houses" on locomotive tenders were for the pleasure of the head brakeman; they were hardly commodious.

Nocturnal slumber in the Alamosa roundhouse
for Rio Grande's narrow-gauge locomotives
was perfectly appropriate, but in the wee
hours of the morning fires would be lit
and these old warriors called to duty.

OFF THE MAIN LINES

K-37 498 and K-36 488 have the duty
this day, highballing through Romeo
with a long train of mixed freight.

Both locomotives are working hard to lug tonnage southward near Romeo but are relaxing over the Conejos River bridge north of Antonito.

In some instances trains were built and then sent to the South Yard in Alamosa, where road power and helper were sent for the pickup.

Pilot-mounted plows suggest the nature of mountain railroading in the snowy season. No snow anywhere this warm day as Mikado 488 leads the way south of La Jara.

The average annual rainfall in much of the San Luis Valley is a mere seven inches, but areas of the valley subject to irrigation produce abundant agricultural produce. Near Romeo.

Only twenty-nine miles separated Alamosa and Antonito, but both locomotives needed to replenish their tanks at Antonito. In the distance, where once the "Chili Line" headed onward to Santa Fe, stands a cut of standard-gauge cars just beyond D&RGW's attractive depot.

Rio Grande's route from Alamosa to Antonito appeared categorically flat, but there was a gradual escalation in elevation. West of Antonito, however, there would be heavy lifting. Ahead, only 11.5 miles, was Lava tank, and in that short distance both locomotives would evaporate enough water to require replenishment.

The fireman is off his seat box – again; 488's firebox seemed to have an insatiable appetite for fuel. No stokers here – every lump of coal had to be shoveled. Just east of Sublette, New Mexico.

On this day, K-37 492 will be in the lead out of Alamosa. To the right is the "boneyard," which often yielded parts to keep other locomotives going. To the left are diesels assigned to local switching chores and runs up the Creede Branch and down to Antonito.

Helper tucked in about mid-train, 492 is ready to head today's drag west out of Antonito. K-37s like 492 had begun life as standard-gauge 2–8–0s, rebuilt into narrow-gauge 2–8–2s by skilled shopmen at Rio Grande's Burnham Shops in Denver.

Struggling upward, ever upward, on a winding, turning, churning right of way, the train already has breached the Colorado–New Mexico border more than a half-dozen times as it wends its way methodically toward Cumbres Pass.

A lone tree seems a sentinel along this horseshoe curve just east of Sublette, New Mexico.

The helper on westbound trains was cut out at Cumbres and proceeded light down to Chama, the train following after it had been inspected and retainers set up to facilitate safe handling on the steep descending grade to Chama. On the next day, crews would be called to move eastbound tonnage from Chama and the west up the sharp escarpment to Cumbres in short chunks. About to leave Chama. Note rotary snowplow at left.

Sublette, 54.4 miles from Alamosa, was a place to clean the fires and refill the tanks of both locomotives, and a place for crewmen to dig into their lunch pails. Water bags hanging from cab windows were a regular feature.

The heavy grade toward Cumbres began almost immediately beyond the yard limits of Chama. It will take the full exertion of both locomotives to lift even a short cut of cars up to Cumbres. K-37s were rated at 252 tons on this stretch, K-36s only 232 tons.

The fireman on the helper is hard at work as the train struggles against the grade and over Lobato Trestle. He and the fireman ahead on the lead locomotive will have no respite for another hour or so.

A spectacular sight and sound of adhesion railroading. Near Cresco, New Mexico.

One long blast of the whistle
signal: "Station One Mile."

OFF THE MAIN LINES

D&RGW operating practice demanded the helpers on Cumbres turns be cut in just ahead of the caboose. Near Coxo, Colorado.

Aaaahh! The sweet taste of success: Cumbres Summit, elevation 10,015. This cut will be set out. Crews will turn both locomotives and caboose on the snowshed-protected wye, and then the engines (one light locomotive, the other toting the cabooses) will head back to Chama to pick up another cut. The entire exercise will be repeated until all east cars have been wrestled up to Cumbres. Finally, all cuts will be gathered into a single train with a maximum of seventy cars, equipment inspected, and air tested.

Doubleheading from Cumbres to Alamosa was not permitted; the helper drifted alone back to the Alamosa terminal. Light engine 488 meets the southbound Antonito turn on the three-rail line at La Jara, about midway between Antonito and Alamosa.

Racing for home, the light engine – the helper – just south of Alamosa. Famous Mount Blanca stands guard over the San Luis Valley to the left.

Trailing its light engine helper by an hour or more, K-37 492 heads its train of company coal, empty boxes, and Gramps tank cars north of La Jara.

On another day, K-36 487 handles a train of mostly Gramps tanks loaded with crude oil for the refinery at Alamosa. K-36s were rated at 1,615 tons between Antonito and Alamosa. Near La Fruto.

The sun is setting to the west as 492 prepares to drop her train in Alamosa's South Yard. It has been a long day.

Slumber well earned. The day crew will drop the fires and put these venerable soldiers into the house on the morrow. Then it will be preparation for the next call.

A trip back to the narrow gauge in 1965 finds a westbound freight pounding along near Monero, New Mexico, with tonnage for Durango and later west of Ignacio, Colorado. An eastbound passenger excursion with Rio Grande's finest equipment struts down the rail near Arboles, Colorado.

D&RGW's carmen at Alamosa. They received little recognition, but with the boilermakers and machinists in the roundhouse, they held the company's increasingly fragile narrow-gauge operation together with perspiration, grit, and baling wire.

Short-line San Luis Central Railroad fed freight traffic from its fifteen-mile line to Rio Grande's Creede Branch at Monte Vista. It was a sleepy interchange for much of the year, but in season, significant tonnage came in the form of lettuce and potatoes.

Twilight comes to the San Luis Valley. Tonnage off the Creede Branch heading for the Alamosa terminal. June 17, 1967.

The long string of empty boxes behind the drawbar of twin SD-9s suggest the grain-based centrality of Milwaukee Road's traffic west of Albert Lea. SD-9s were rated at 1,750 hp. Westbound near Armstrong, fall 1968.

A MOVE TO ALBERT LEA IN SOUTH-CENTRAL MINNE-
sota offered a fresh vantage point from which to view the
rapidly changing railroad landscape in the second half of the
1960s.

A Chicago, Milwaukee, St. Paul & Pacific (CMStP&P or
Milwaukee Road) predecessor had pioneered railroad transportation in the area with a horizontal-axis route that led
from the Mississippi River at La Crescent through Albert Lea
to Wells in 1866–70 and later pushed completely across the
southern part of the state and into Dakota Territory. In 1907,
Milwaukee Road also completed a forty-mile feeder from Albert Lea northwestward to St. Clair.

Second on the scene was Minneapolis & St. Louis
(M&StL), which reached Albert Lea in 1877. Three years later,
it had punched on southwestward to reach Fort Dodge, Iowa.
Eventually, it cobbled together a through route from Minneapolis and St. Paul to Des Moines via Albert Lea, which,
in the process, was vested as a crew-change point with active
yarding chores.

M&StL entered into important financial and operating
arrangements with Burlington, Cedar Rapids & Northern
(BCR&N), which resulted in a complicated agreement that
brought BCR&N into Albert Lea from the south and, with
additional alliances with Chicago, Rock Island & Pacific
(CRI&P or Rock Island) and Chicago, Burlington & Quincy
(CB&Q or Burlington Route), opened an important chute
from Minneapolis and St. Paul to Chicago and St. Louis. Even
before it became an integral part of Rock Island, BCR&N ini-
tiated construction of its own independent route north from
Albert Lea to the Twin Cities, with Rock Island completing
that strategic arm in 1902 and thereby abrogating earlier arrangements with M&StL.

This new wrinkle produced its own wave of change.
M&StL gained control of Iowa Central, which in 1901 began
to operate trains into Albert Lea from the south. M&StL a decade later merged the two properties, and with a Wabash connection at Albia, Iowa Central continued to maintain a Minneapolis–St. Louis traffic option. In addition, Illinois Central
(IC) extended an existing branch from Waterloo a few miles to
Glenville, Minnesota, and by way of trackage rights, entered
the Albert Lea arena in 1900. IC yarded its trains with M&StL
and the two roads quickly agreed to move traffic jointly in the
Twin Cities–Albert Lea–Waterloo–Chicago corridor.

: : :

Milwaukee Road carded a daily-except-Sunday freight in each direction from Austin to Jackson through Albert Lea. A mix of Alco and Electro-Motive Division power has a roll on train 203's extra through Hayward, the first station east of Albert Lea. September 1966.

The action at Milwaukee Road's depot site at Albert Lea this summer afternoon in 1968 gives the aura of casualness, but the switch crew shortly will head for the large Wilson & Company packing plant to dig out loads of meat that will head east on train 222.

Motive power assigned to trains 203 and 222 was predictably eclectic, but Albert Lea winters were utterly predictable – cold and snowy. Train 203 heads by the depot. Work Extra 517, in the hole, has cleared the line to the west. March 1967.

All 3,100 horses of combined Alco–EMD power are fully engaged in lugging train 203 through Alden, eleven miles west of **Albert Lea.** April 11, 1970.

Maximum authorized speed was thirty-five miles per hour on the Austin–Jackson line, and to maintain that possibility, track had to be properly maintained–which was increasingly problematic at Milwaukee, but on this hot summer morning in 1969, crews spread ballast near Hollandale Junction.

With cab controls reversed so that the short end of the locomotive has become the front end Alco RSD-5 573 with EMD SD-7 in support hoists train 203 up grade out of Albert Lea to the west. April 11, 1970.

The three reefers on the point of train 222 derive from the Wilson & Company meatpacking plant at Albert Lea and will be combined at Austin with tonnage coming from the George A. Hormel plant, then hustled to the Indiana Harbor Belt interchange near Chicago for Eastern Seaboard destinations. Scurrying along just behind 222 comes the Albert Lea switch job heading back to its Austin terminal with but one car and caboose. Mid-July 1970, near Oakland, ten miles from Austin, fourteen miles from Albert Lea.

The URTX car on the point of this Sunday extra is headed up the St. Clair branch to Waldorf, where it will take on 10,000 pounds of butter churned by the local creamery and billed to eastern markets. Ahead lay snow-filled cuts soon cleared by the wedge plow pushed on by SD-7 513. Between Freeborn and Matawan, January 1967.

The St. Clair branch jutted northwest a mile west of the Albert Lea depot. No open stations remained on the line, and service was irregular, usually once or twice weekly. Extra 955 West buzzes along at twenty miles per hour near Freeborn on a Saturday afternoon in September 1966.

Chicago & North Western train 1, up from Marshalltown, Iowa, with former-M&StL GP-9s as power, has come off the joint track (CRI&P and C&NW Manly–Albert Lea, and IC also from Glenville) and is about to cross Rock Island's branch from Estherville, Iowa, before heading into the Albert Lea Yard. Notice the empty CB&Q stock cars on the point. April 1967.

No. 20's extra is on joint track just south of Albert Lea with a long train of mixed freight headed by an assortment of power: ex-M&StL, ex-Great Western, and C&NW. Summer 1969.

After Chicago Great Western became part of the C&NW empire in 1968, former CGW power appeared frequently at Albert Lea on what once had been M&StL. Crews have changed, and train 20 eases ahead toward the CMStP&P crossing and then to the joint track that will take it to Manly, Iowa, and home rail again all the way to Peoria, Illinois. January 1969.

Rock Island's Minneapolis–Des Moines–Kansas City route through Albert Lea was fully signaled and in 1966 still featured six passenger trains daily. Flagship was the *Plainsman*, successor to the *Twin Star Rocket*. It still had an attractive diner and through deluxe coach between Minneapolis and Los Angeles via Kansas City. Train 17 with a six-car consist slows to a stop before Rock Island's attractive depot. September 1967.

Rock Island's Hollandale branch peeled away from the main line above Albert Lea at Clarks Grove to serve shippers at West Side, Hollandale, and Maple Island. The sugar-beet harvest at Hollandale was in full flower this splendid day in September 1966. Extra 1303 is about to pull out with about thirty cars of beets for the American Crystal Sugar refinery at Mason City, Iowa.

Rock Island's train 17 leaving Albert Lea on its run to Kansas City. In the foreground is Rock Island's "Bug Line" from Estherville at the crossing of C&NW's line from the joint track to its yard.

Burlington Route in Albert Lea? No, but CB&Q and CRI&P jointly sponsored what until recently had been the *Zephyr-Rocket*, by March 1967 without name and soon to be discontinued, yet still with a mix of motive power and equipment from both roads. Train 20 leaving town, headed for St. Paul and Minneapolis.

Illinois Central pride into and out of Albert Lea were trains 571 and 572, symbol trains CA1 and AC2, joint operations with C&NW expediting freight between the Twin Cities and Chicago via Albert Lea and Waterloo. Down from Minneapolis and off the joint track from Albert Lea, IC's AC2 is on home rail at Glenville. M&StL and IC had a power-sharing agreement that was continued with C&NW. AC2 will make no stops on its hundred-mile jaunt to Waterloo. August 1966.

The Hollandale Turn on this bitterly cold January day in 1970 has six empty refrigerator cars requested by potato and onion shippers at Hollandale. During the annual nine-month shipping season, customers billed locally grown potatoes as well as those from the distant Red River Valley for washing and packing.

Heavy wind-blown snow to foul cuts presented all area railroads with an annual operating headache. Protocols varied among them as to clearing lines. M&StL and then C&NW typically called out snowplow extras like this one resting briefly in the Albert Lea Yard. Note the mixed parentage of plows and locomotives. January 1970.

In addition to its premier trains, IC also scheduled tri-weekly local service to and from Albert Lea with trains 591 and 592. Here is 592 on joint track between Albert Lea and Glenville on a frigid early morning in January 1970.

IC chose to put a wedge plow on its tri-weekly local in order to open or keep open its Waterloo–Glenville line. On the joint track south of Albert Lea, January 1969.

Rock Island's busy main route through Albert Lea was hardly immune from snow problems. Hitting drifts at high speed was a real show for onlookers, but it must have created mixed feelings among those in locomotive cabs and the trailing cabooses. Between Albert Lea and Clarks Grove, January 1969.

Job done. The Milwaukee branch to St. Clair has been cleared upbound, and now wedge plow and flanger are tucked into the train for the return trip to Albert Lea. Between Waldorf and Matawan. It is Super Bowl Sunday, 1969. The crew, greatly interested in the outcome of the game and devoted in their collective disdain for "Broadway" Joe Namath and the New York Jets, has no radio, but the photographer does. The train thus stopped every so many miles to get an update. News for the crew was utterly depressing: the Jets won 16 to 7 over the Baltimore Colts, and Namath was named Most Valuable Player.

Change was afoot. Big change. And rapid. Passenger-train discontinuances, the closing of country depots, line abandonments, mergers, and creation of holding companies all were part of the mix as the railroad industry struggled to right itself against the heavy hand of government regulations; archaic work rules; often-inept management; and tax-supported, competitive modes of transportation. All of it was reflected close at hand and abroad the land.

Chicago Great Western sported main routes serving Chicago, Minneapolis–St. Paul, Kansas City, and Council Bluffs–Omaha, but it was a latecomer to upper Midwest sweepstakes and suffered accordingly because others had better chosen routes and better developed sources of traffic. Great Western also had a few generally unremarked branches, necessary and useful in an earlier time, but increasingly suspect in an era of intense modal competition. Line abandonments accelerated with predictable frequency. CGW made its final sojourn in Iowa from McIntire to Osage on April 10, 1967, with but one final carload to an Osage customer. Rails were ripped out shortly thereafter.

The Cedar Falls branch erupted from Great Western's Oelwein–Des Moines–Kansas City artery at appropriately named Cedar Falls Junction. CGW had a good customer base at Cedar Falls, but elderly EMD switcher no. 6 spent much of its time slumbering before the depot. June 1967.

CGW way freight 121 en route from Red Wing, Minnesota, to Mankato has a respectable train as it trundles westward on this pleasant May morning in 1967. Approaching the Rock Island crossing above Faribault. The line once had been independent and then came under control of Minneapolis & St. Louis. Great Western gathered it to its corporate bosom in 1899.

Country depots like Great Western's at Meservey, Iowa, were increasingly anachronistic with the demise of passenger trains and less-than-carload freight business. They were closed in droves during the 1960s.

Cold and lonely, CGW's Alco-led caboose hop putters slowly toward Faribault, Minnesota, in January 1968. Great Western would not see another winter.

Chicago, Burlington & Quincy's train 43 at Gillette, Wyoming, was 652 miles and fourteen hours and forty-five minutes from its Omaha starting point. A Pullman sleeping car (four sections, six roomettes, four double bedrooms) was still assigned between Omaha and Alliance. It was typically a single chair car for the duration of the trip to Billings, Montana. Gillette was a meal stop, but few on this drizzly June 12, 1967, chose to walk a few blocks to a local beanery.

By the mid-1960s, most agents at country stations had little to do and welcomed a stranger who happened by and wanted to visit about railroading in yesteryear. Certainly, that was the case for Northern Pacific's wonderfully accommodating veteran agent at Hitterdal, Minnesota. Here he demonstrates how it had been "in the old days" to hand up orders or messages to passing trains in the night. September 15, 1967.

185

Burlington Route passenger service on the Omaha–Billings run, at least from Lincoln to Billings, was already living on borrowed time, but its death sentence was assured when the Post Office Department ended its contract for service on the route. Train 42 "waits for time" – it cannot leave before scheduled departure – at Clearmont, Wyoming, July 12, 1968. Without mail-handling chores, trains were frequently ahead of schedule upon arrival at en-route stopping points.

Note the nine cars of livestock on the point of this CB&Q manifest freight hurrying eastward near Ulm, Wyoming, behind three GE units on July 12, 1968.

A harbinger of things to come. Burlington Route Extra 363 East labors near Moorcroft, Wyoming, with a trainload of low-sulfur coal on July 12, 1968. Nobody would yet dream of the huge future expansion of coal extraction from the Powder River Basin.

Rock Island whittled passenger service on its "Choctaw Route" from Memphis, Tennessee, to Tucumcari, New Mexico, to a single sortie in each direction. It handled mostly mail, which it handed to and received from Southern Pacific at Tucumcari, in this way linking Memphis with Los Angeles. CRI&P, in an offhand or "make do" spirit, employed RDCs (dead in train) to handle the RPO assignment and occasional passengers. Train 22 arriving at and leaving Amarillo, Texas, June 20, 1967.

Noon at Forest Lake, Minnesota, on Northern Pacific's St. Paul–Twin Ports (Skally) line. NP's track rider has left his speeder (motorcar) on the main line long enough for a short visit with the local agent and to secure a line-up of trains that he must look out for on his afternoon sojourn. May 1964.

Rock Island's daily-except-Sunday freight rumbles eastward over the East Fork of the Des Moines River near Armstrong, Iowa, with empty grain boxes for distribution to on-line elevators as well as meat from an Estherville packing plant that will be hurried on to destination from Albert Lea, Minnesota.

By 1967, Northern Pacific's passenger service between the Twin Cities and Winnipeg, Manitoba, required a change of trains at Hawley, Minnesota—NP's *Mainstreeter* to and from Minneapolis and St. Paul and an RDC from Hawley to Winnipeg. No. 1 rolling into Hawley from the east, no. 13 on the other track. September 15, 1967.

Chicago & North Western continued to operate a number of branches on its expansive upper-Midwestern system. One of these in Minnesota was thirty-four miles from Blue Earth to Lake Crystal. The branch lived on grain moved in boxcars, but certain demise was in the offing. Northbound above Blue Earth, May 1968.

NP's route to the Canadian boundary meandered north from Hawley to Crookston and then pointed to Grand Forks, North Dakota, hugging the North Dakota–Minnesota border to Pembina (with Canadian National beyond). Train 13 (B-32) purrs along above Hitterdal, Minnesota. Winnipeg was six hours and fifteen minutes away. September 15, 1967.

Until mail contracts ended on October 18, 1967, NP combined trains 3 and 11 between St. Paul and Little Falls, with train 3 continuing on to Mandan, North Dakota, and train 11 pushing on north to Bemidji and then northeast to International Falls. Subsequent to the loss of mail, however, NP discontinued train 3 entirely and train 11 from St. Paul to Little Falls, assigning an RDC to the now-isolated and disconnected remainder of the run to and from International Falls. Not surprisingly, passengers were few. Train 11 left Little Falls at 1:45 AM; train 12 returned at 11:22 PM. Little Falls, July 9, 1968.

Minneapolis, Northfield & Southern carved out an existence by offering on-line customers high quality and reliable service and especially by expediting interchange traffic – serving as a bridge carrier – between the west side of Minneapolis and the south side of Minneapolis to Northfield, forty-five miles. Center cab Baldwin 23 got the call this March day in 1969 to clear the line of snow. Job done, the crew could take a break at Northfield.

Despite the loss of mail revenue, Union Pacific continued to offer passenger service on the 397-mile route linking Salt Lake City, Utah, with Butte, Montana. The train ran only on a tri-weekly schedule, but a sleeper–snack bar car (four sections, six roomettes, four double bedrooms and a tiny snack–beverage service area) remained part of the consist. Departure from Butte was at 7:30 PM. June 6, 1969.

193

Sioux City Terminal (SCT) provided important switching service in and about the stockyards and packing houses of that western-Iowa city, but major changes in the meat business and in the location of new processing plants elsewhere put a long shadow on SCT. September 28, 1969.

Chicago, Milwaukee, St. Paul & Pacific played a dominant role in railroad transportation across the southern portion of Minnesota. An important branch reached up from Wells to traffic-rich Mankato. Milwaukee Road provided daily-except-Sunday freight service in both directions. Train 561 with Alco RSD-5 570 has just left Minnesota Lake, August 1966.

CMStP&P train 64 rumbles southward near Medford, Minnesota, with a long string of empty boxcars on Milwaukee Road's pioneer line that opened service to St. Paul and Minneapolis from the east more than a century earlier. July 1970.

Canadian National's Extra 5038 East has a long drag of mixed freight as it eases into Warroad, Minnesota. June 8, 1970.

Canadian National's Port Arthur, Ontario–Winnipeg, Manitoba, line clipped extreme northern Minnesota from Baudette to Warroad, 36.4 miles. CN scheduled tri-weekly passenger service, providing a snack coach for the convenience of customers. Train 192 at the Minnesota–Manitoba boundary for customs inspection and at Roosevelt. June 8, 1970.

Illinois Central's *Hawkeye* had been a staple in that road's passenger offerings between Chicago and Sioux City. As late as 1953, it had featured up to ten head-end cars, three coaches, a buffet–lounge, and two sleepers. By September 1969, when this study was made of train 12 just before its departure from Sioux City, it was down to only coaches for passengers. The Sioux City sleeper had run its final miles at the end of April 1968.

By now shorn of its sleeper, IC's *Hawkeye* in May 1969 still handled an RPO car (that was manned and worked only between Chicago and Fort Dodge). No. 12 works its way eastward near James, Iowa. The train's veteran conductor sold fewer and fewer cash fares as travelers increasingly found other means of transportation.

The sun was rising in the east as IC's *Hawkeye* blows through Tara, just west of Fort Dodge, Iowa, on April 27, 1968, but in a very real way, the sun was setting on much that had been typical in the railroad industry for decades. It was a long track looking back.

Phyllis Rainbolt was Santa Fe's agent at Kaw, Oklahoma. After the final trains passed that station on December 10, 1971, her services there were no longer required, and Track Supervisor Floyd E. Reisch would no longer need to monitor Santa Fe's right-of-way from Newkirk to Burbank – track soon to be covered with lake water created by the new dam nearby.

EDUCATIONAL OPPORTUNITY AT OKLAHOMA STATE University presented itself during the first portion of the 1970s. Stillwater was Atchison, Topeka & Santa Fe (AT&SF or Santa Fe) country, located on a spur from what once had been a concave but through route from Newkirk, Oklahoma, to Pauls Valley, Oklahoma, parallel to the east of Santa Fe's main gut from Newton, Kansas, to the Gulf of Mexico. Passenger service had ended November 10, 1956, but local customers still provided attractive freight revenue.

Santa Fe was a well-managed company with premier routes from Chicago to Los Angeles and Chicago to South Texas. In a relative sense, it was prosperous compared to many other railroads at the time. Yet the mood across the industry was grim, and it got worse as the decade of the 1970s wore on. Causes of financial anemia were many and varied among particular companies, but a popular prescription among virtually all carriers was abandonment of line segments, especially branches and redundant secondary routes. Santa Fe was not immune in this regard.

The Arkansas River was a traditional source of difficulty for AT&SF between Newkirk and Burbank whenever its banks were swollen with the runoff of spring thaws or the result of sudden thunderstorms. To eradicate these problems, the United States Army Corps of Engineers was authorized to build a dam on the Arkansas near Kaw that would inundate a huge chunk of land through which Santa Fe's Newkirk–Pauls Valley line passed. Abandonment of that twenty-five-mile piece from Newkirk to Burbank was required, and Santa Fe had little objection. In the process, the company terminated through service on its side-by-side, north–south route via Fairfax, Cushing, and Shawnee. Abandonment proceedings that were the result of flood-control needs were, of course, an exception. Usually such applications sprang from accumulated economic causes.

That certainly was the case for cash-starved Missouri–Kansas–Texas (M–K–T or Katy), which in 1969 applied to the Interstate Commerce Commission (ICC) for authority to abandon its entire operation above Altus, Oklahoma – 331 miles along the western boundary of the state and across the Panhandle, including all of its wholly owned Beaver, Meade & Englewood (BM&E). Indeed, the matter made Oklahoma the epicenter of the railroad industry's rush to shed itself of unwanted route miles. And, given the magnitude and complexity of the application, the ICC would spend a protracted time studying the issue. In the end, as might be expected, Katy was successful; the ICC's decision resulted in the longest single branch-line abandonment ever to that time.

The enterprise derived from the dreams of Texas entrepreneurs who had envisioned a rail system that would hold a huge portion of the new state of Oklahoma to the economic interests of Wichita Falls. Thus was born the Wichita Falls & Northwestern (WF&N), which in the period 1906–12 pushed rail upward and over the Red River, angling northwest to Altus, then north to Mangum, Elk City, and Woodward before pressing westward into the Panhandle and terminating at Forgan. BM&E, which Katy eventually acquired, extended from Forgan across the Panhandle to Keyes, the last outpost on the far frontier of Katy's domain, in 1915–31. There were good times: the Burkburnett oil boom and the years of bountiful harvest. There were bad times: the Depression and the Dust Bowl. Fortunes seemed to even out. But M–K–T fell on hard times during the late 1950s and early 1960s. Maintenance was slashed, service suffered, customers decamped. All of it was reflected starkly on Katy's Northwestern District and BM&E. Scarce resources understandably flowed into M–K–T's main routes; the Northwestern District and BM&E were expendable.

AT&SF's Stillwater depot was typical of many other structures around the system and seemed to imply the company's overarching mantra: solid, prosperous, permanent.

Big-time railroading lurked nearby in the form of AT&SF's
main route through Oklahoma to and from Texas. The star
attraction was Santa Fe's sleek *Texas Chief*. It honored Perry
with a daily northbound dinnertime stop, where genial
ticket agent–operator Dayton Webb handled all the chores
with efficiency, grace and charm. Sandra and Kathryn
Hofsommer admire one of Santa Fe's finest. April 1971.

About fifty people turned out to greet the final southbound train at Kaw. The crew willingly spent about thirty minutes being "honored" and then it was off to finish the run.

The Missouri–Kansas–Texas main route from St. Louis and Kansas City to Dallas, Fort Worth, and beyond ran diagonally across eastern Oklahoma from north to south. From it sprang a secondary route that served Bartlesville, Cushing, and Oklahoma City. A downbound drag rumbled through Cushing at noontide on a bright Saturday early in September 1970.

Katy's engine facility at Oklahoma City was, well, functional. June 1973.

Engineer Byron Bates eases Extra 101 East beneath stately Chinese elm trees near historic Fort Supply and then out of the hills and onto the flats west of Woodward on Katy's Northwestern District. October 1971.

By the fall of 1971, track conditions on the Northwestern District meant that locomotives, equipment, and crews could expect that six days would be required to make a round trip from Wichita Falls to Forgan and back. Locomotives tied up in front of the depot at Woodward with engines running, much to the annoyance of nearby residents. October 1971.

Agent P. A. Johnson corrects the setting on the standard clock at Katy's Elk City depot. It was November 30, 1971, his retirement day.

Day five in a six-day cycle saw tonnage move from Woodward to Altus, 144 miles. Extra 117 East moves along gingerly – maximum authorized speed, fifteen miles per hour – between Woodward and Sharon. October 1971.

Katy management had anticipated permission-to-abandon before the 1972 wheat harvest, but they got it wrong. There were other complications with the result that operating conditions were worse than ever. BM&E could have used a combine like the one harvesting wheat at left to "harvest" weeds that completely obliterated the track. Substantial grain elevators at Hough are in view to the west, but the train would be a long time getting there. June 28, 1972.

Katy passed through picturesque rolling country be-tween Leedey and Trail. Extra 112 West pads lightly. Tie conditions were deplorable. The bulkhead flat ahead of the caboose carries ties, rail, spikes, angle bars and tools. Better to be prepared – derailments were expected.

Track conditions abroad the Northwestern District were appreciably worse in 1972 than just a year earlier. Six-day cycles between Wichita Falls and Forgan became a mirage. The station sign at Trail was a metaphor for the woebegone nature of Katy's property. June 30, 1972.

Conditions on BM&E were no better, often worse. Conductor L. E. Smith (if necessary, he could fill in as either brakeman or engineer – BM&E operations were "casual") opens the gate against traffic on Rock Island's Golden State Route at Hooker, June 28, 1972. Smith and Engineer T. J. Robb were in for a long slog out to Keyes and back.

Morning was completely consumed in making the forty miles from Forgan to Hooker. Time for lunch before pressing west.

It took all the patience and talent of a savvy and experienced T. J. Robb to drag his train of empty grain boxes through a sea of vegetation covering a very delicate track structure. An itinerant field mouse moving parallel with the train at tie ends makes better time. The mouse, either frightened or with an acute competitive instinct, soon outdistances the train. June 28, 1972.

Extra 112 West rumbles out of Hovey Cut into Goff Creek bottoms late in the afternoon of June 28, 1972. Note the no. 2 track shovel behind the grab irons of the locomotive. In a few minutes, Extra 112 will stall in deep weeds on the upgrade west of Goff Creek. That shovel and others then would be employed by track laborers, who scooped sand onto the rails in an attempt to improve traction. It proved a frustrating day for veteran BM&E employees who recalled better times.

Track laborers shadowing the struggling train were called on to scare up sand to replenish the locomotive's reservoir. Indeed, Engineer T. J. Robb found it necessary to run the sanders almost constantly over rails made extremely slippery by crushed weeds. Eva, June 29, 1972.

A time-honored tradition, hardly necessary on BM&E, Robb and Smith compare watches. In any event, it was 7:00 AM – time to leave Keyes, trailing only the bulkhead ("track equipment") flat and caboose. Ahead at the next several stations wait boxcars heavily laden with wheat to be moved east. July 26, 1972.

Loads have been picked up at Eva and more will be added at Hough and other stations. Edging by the dilapidated signboard at Muncy, July 26, 1972.

Not all of Katy's Northwestern District fell to the wreckers. Frank W. Pollock Jr. acquired 3.3 miles of main track and all of Katy's yard and sidings at Woodward. His Northwestern Oklahoma (NOKL) would offer former Katy customers personally tailored service – cars interchanged to and from AT&SF. Little looks at big. Santa Fe Extra 5661 East as seen from NOKL's no. 1, a GE center cab. April 1976.

On the ground – again – at milepost 51, between Mouser and Hooker. November 10, 1972.

OFF THE MAIN LINES

The end came, as it had to, in January 1973. BM&E ran its final miles on the 10th. Two days later, Extra 98 East rattled out of Forgan for Woodward. A variety of delays postponed the last sortie from Woodward until the 24th. Rolling along slowly between Trail and Leedey, Extra 98 presents a melancholy scene – a solitary steer paying absolutely no respect to the funeral cortege.

On June 19, 1976, Pollock hosted a "rolling autograph party" on his NOKL to introduce *Katy Northwest: The Story of Branch Line Railroad.* Honored guest was John W. Barriger, former M–K–T president and the industry's prominent elder statesman.

Katy earlier had jettisoned most of Northwestern District's Wellington branch, which jutted west from **Altus to Wellington, Texas.** But Hollis & Eastern (H&E) was formed to acquire and operate the line from Altus to Hollis, 33.4 miles. The grain elevator at Victory promised H&E substantial wheat tonnage in harvest season. June 19, 1978.

Pollock operated his little railroad, "The Red Carpet Line," for profit and for fun, too. October 1976.

Arrival of the *Freedom Train* at Wichita Falls on March 6, 1976, caused considerable excitement within that community but considerable heartburn for Katy officials who had to oversee handling of the train. Kids eagerly sought to retrieve coins pressed flat by Southern Pacific's famous 4–8–4 4449 and Katy's 109. Shoving into Sheppard Air Force Base.

Katy retained a major presence at Wichita Falls, but by this time the company had reached the city from Fort Worth not by its own rail but by operating rights over Fort Worth & Denver (FtW&D, Burlington Northern). An up-train rolls into North Yard. The switch crew at left soon will disassemble the train and deliver cars to local customers. January 1976.

M–K–T still owned the seventy-seven-mile line from Wichita Falls to Altus that could be depended on to furnish appreciable business when crops were good. Katy modestly upgraded the track, but speeds remained restricted to ten miles per hour. The brakeman offers a friendly wave as this long drag of wheat-laden boxcars lumbers south between Burkburnett and Wichita Falls. March 6, 1976.

Santa Fe's north–south line serving Plainview
acted as something of a connector between
two of the company's primary east–west lines.
A southbound manifest freight slows down
but will not stop at Plainview. April 1980.

WORK OPPORTUNITY AT PLAINVIEW, TEXAS, PRE-sented itself in 1973 and would result in a fourteen-year stay in the Lone Star State. Plainview, like Stillwater in Oklahoma, was Atchison, Topeka & Santa Fe (AT&SF or Santa Fe) coun-try, served, as it was, by a primary north–south line linking Amarillo and Lubbock, completed in 1907–10, and a stub southeastward to Floydada, twenty-seven miles, in 1910. Fort Worth & Denver (FTW&D or Denver) also occupied the terri-tory in 1929 with an extension from its Amarillo–Fort Worth main at Estelline to Lubbock, with a spur to Plainview and on northwest to Dimmitt.

Still another aspirant in the region was Quanah, Acme & Pacific (QA&P or Quanah Route), which, in fits and starts (1903–1909), pushed a line of road west from Quanah to Pa-ducah and finally to Floydada (1929). St. Louis–San Francisco's (SL–SF's or Frisco's) western reach from St. Louis and Kansas City through Tulsa and Oklahoma City stubbed at Quanah. Predictably, Frisco took an interest in and then took control of QA&P as a logical extension of its strategic aspirations. In time, and for several years, Frisco and Santa Fe teamed on long-distance, expedited traffic moving over the Floydada Gate-way. Indeed, QLA and QSF were a couple of Frisco's hottest freights; they were authorized forty-nine miles per hour across QA&P's 110-mile route between Quanah and Floydada. But in 1973, Frisco and Santa Fe agreed to move their joint business up to the Avard Gateway in Oklahoma, and QA&P faced an uncertain future. Local business ebbed and flowed, but mostly ebbed. Abandonment was sought and permission gained, at least west of Paducah to Floydada, sixty-seven miles. The final run was made on May 5, 1981.

The train-order signal is clear for this north-bound manifest at Kress on a crisp December day in 1976. Santa Fe's country depot was as classy as it was utilitarian.

Santa Fe had major customers at Plainview. These included Midwest Grain, which did its own switching with a former AT&SF center-cab goat. April 1978.

Tulia, twenty-five miles above Plainview, offered Santa Fe considerable traffic from local shippers. Tulia Wheat Growers handles its own switching chores. Spring 1980.

Not surprisingly, grain – wheat and milo, in particular – provided major sources of revenue from stations in this part of Santa Fe's domain. A southbound extra has just picked up a few cars from one of the elevators at Kress, the first station north of Plainview. July 1, 1978.

Most of the tonnage on this Santa Fe drag pounding over the Burlington Northern (FW&D) diamond at Lockney, Texas, is headed for the QA&P interchange at Floydada. August 1975

Traffic dwindled considerably on Santa Fe's branch from Plainview to Floydada after through business was diverted to the Avard Gateway. On this day in early May 1981, there are two carloads of machinery to be delivered at Lockney.

Power assigned to Burlington Northern's Fort Worth & Denver line into and out of Plainview was uniformly stocked with EMD six-axle units. Heading for Plainview, east of town, August 1, 1973.

OFF THE MAIN LINES

The merger of several corporate entities to form Burlington Northern had occurred in 1970, but it would take time to put all motive power and rolling stock through paint shops to emerge with new corporate colors. These two SD-7s and caboose readying for an assignment at Plainview, however, are shiny with Cascade green and white adornment. May 1974.

FtW&D often called a daily-except-Sunday turn from Plainview to Dimmitt, site of a large corn wet-milling plant and a very good customer. The outside-frame wooden caboose, a regular for years, soon would disappear. August 2, 1973.

With the sweet smell of home in his nostrils, the engineer on this eastbound Saturday afternoon return from Dimmitt hurries his train through Hart, twenty-seven miles from Plainview. The unused water tank in the background remained a physical reminder of railroad need and practice now obsolete. This 37.5-mile line would be sold to a short-line operator in 2007. December 1973.

Trackmen on this speeder ("putt-putt car") are about to enter the darkness of FtW&D's tunnel near Quitaque. They must have wondered as to the sanity of some itinerant photographer. "Watch out for snakes!" August 1974.

Picking up ten loads of wheat. Boothe Spur, January 20, 1976.

232

After through business was diverted to the Avard Gateway in 1973, QA&P initially worked a crew six days per week on Floydada turns from Quanah. Boxcars in the yard at Floydada will in time be loaded with cotton bales from the local gin. January 20, 1976.

Land east of Floydada to the Caprock was good for grazing cattle, but also for the production of cereal grains, especially wheat. Dougherty is in the distance. January 20, 1976.

Coming off the Caprock into "boot-and-saddle" country near MacBain. January 20, 1976.

Demand for transportation varied by season and by vacillations in the local and national economies. QA&P varied crew starts accordingly, with trains running to Floydada only once a week in some instances. The movement of wallboard to California markets from Acme remained relatively strong, with empties coming back in reverse routing from AT&SF to Floydada. On this day, Extra 500 East had only five empty bulkhead flats for Acme out of Floydada and nothing to pick up at Dougherty, in the background. May 1977.

Five carloads of cotton bales have been added at Roaring Springs. Here, the train is passing Russellville, where in an earlier era trainloads of cattle had been loaded with frequency. See remnants of pens and chutes at left. May 1977.

Track conditions remained good, and a single unit was quite adequate to negotiate short grades such as this one near Narcisso. May 1977.

Additional cotton bales in boxcars were added to the consist at Paducah. Swearingen by 1977 claimed only a signboard and a ninety-four-car passing track when it once had boasted a two-story hotel, a hardware store, a grocery store, a cotton gin, a public school, and a handsome frame depot. May 1977.

By the time the sun was setting on Extra 500 East, it had grown to a substantial train of grain, cotton, and empty bulkhead flats. In the Pease River breaks west of Lazare. May 1977.

QA&P in 1929 had promised that it would build "one of the best depots a town the size of Floydada has ever been provided," and it was good to its word. But by 1976, it was unused, silent, empty, a shell. Crews tied up in front of the depot in keeping with tradition as much as anything. January 16, 1976.

Extra 437 East has gathered up a dozen cars of wheat ahead of empty bulkhead flats and glides through Dougherty before slipping down the Caprock's escarpment toward MacBain. January 16, 1976.

There is only one covered hopper loaded with wheat this day, but trackside elevators have nearly emptied their bins in anticipation of the next harvest, only a few days away. Near Dougherty, May 1977.

It is a big country, nearly swallowing up this QA&P intruder near MacBain. May, 1977.

The clock was winding down on QA&P and its employees. Left to right: Clyde King, engineer; Fred Pierce, brakeman; Dee Smith, fireman; William Clawson, conductor; and Larry Tidmore, brakeman. Small wonder there was not a smile among them. Floydada, March 19, 1981.

Roaring Springs once had been a vibrant place, with buildings sprouting up like weeds soon after the railroad arrived. But it withered over time, and the end of rail service suggested further decline. Agency service had ended with the departure of the through trains. Eastbound, March 19, 1981.

242

Except for the generous and gracious chattering of songbirds, it was almost ghostly silent before Extra 1382 East interrupted briefly at 4:25 PM, passing the handsome but silent depot and rolling through Roaring Springs in regal style on well-anchored 115-pound steel with ties deeply bedded in chat ballast. Not even the free whistling of Engineer Clyde H. King brought out a solitary soul to witness the end of an era. Brakeman Larry Tidmore waves a final goodbye and then deserts the back platform to the inside of the caboose as the train rumbles over Shorty Creek trestle and disappears forever around a curve. May 5, 1981.

In the distance is the headlight of AT&SF Extra 3604 East, soon to be about the business of spotting empty boxes at docks formerly served by QA&P in Floydada. The final QA&P train had departed only a few hours earlier. The old order had passed, and the new had begun. 6:00 PM, May 5, 1981.

No QA&P tonnage from the west this day, so Frisco train 3310 to Oklahoma City has only two boxes and a scale test car ahead of its caboose out of Quanah. January 1976.

QA&P's handsome general office and station building at Quanah are behind locomotive 508 and caboose. Power and caboose at right have come in from the east on a Frisco run. February 1977.

Burlington Northern's (née Colorado & Southern [C&S]–Fort Worth & Denver's) route from Denver through Pueblo to Amarillo and Fort Worth never had been dense with freight traffic, but that would change dramatically as demand for Powder River coal escalated. Five hefty units headed by C&S 950 were required for this hauler to lug manifest tonnage over a challenging profile from Colorado through New Mexico and into Texas. Texline, October 1976. That train represented the route's historic mission, but in March 1977, Extra 5829 East represented the new: low-sulfur coal heading for Texas generating plants. Amarillo, March 1977.

Amarillo was a major point on AT&SF's vital cross-country freight main, but also a point from which trains were dispatched in "dark territory" southward to Lubbock and northward to La Junta, Colorado – lines that would see much of the company's first-generation diesel–electric motive power. Note Santa Fe's giant wrecking derrick at right, soon to become an anachronism. March 1977.

Rock Island's (Chicago, Rock Island & Pacific) Choctaw Route from Memphis across Arkansas, Oklahoma, and the Texas Panhandle to a connection with Southern Pacific (SP) at Tucumcari, New Mexico, always was pregnant with strategic possibilities. But that marvelous potential was never achieved, although this lengthy westbound freight rumbling along between Jericho and Groom, Texas, suggests otherwise. Illusions notwithstanding, by March 1977, a single trip daily in each direction would suffice between El Reno, Oklahoma, and Amarillo, except, of course, during harvest season.

A setting sun shines brightly against this heavy Rock Island drag of mixed freight as it rolls by giant grain elevators at Groom. A sense of serenity was utterly deceiving. All was not well at Rock Island. March 1977.

Two freshly painted GP-38s in blue-and-white livery boldly proclaim that there was a new "Rock." Alas, it was not so. Hustling eastward with a dozen cars taken from the SP interchange at Tucumcari and headed for Amarillo. Just beyond Glen Rio and near Adrian, March 1977.

The scene at Rock Island's Amarillo engine terminal on the morning of March 25, 1980, was routine, nothing unusual. But, in fact, Rock Island was taking in its final gasps of oxygen.

Clouds gathered as Extra 4422 West rattled toward Tucumcari from Amarillo. It was one of the final clean-up trains, for the most part getting SP rolling stock back to its owner before the final embargo. West of Adrian, March 25, 1980.

Rock Island had been "a mighty fine line." True enough, but no pleasant melody lingered about it now. The only sound to be heard this day was an ugly death rattle. Soon others would carve parts from its corpse. That which nobody wanted would be abandoned. Such would be the fate of this part of Rock Island's once mighty empire. Westbound making forty-five miles per hour on surprisingly good track in rough country between Adrian and Glen Rio. March 25, 1980.

Roscoe, Snyder & Pacific (RS&P) earned a sterling reputation among shippers as a "fast and dependable through traffic route between the Pacific Coast and the East," serving, as it did, as a bridge carrier between Texas & Pacific (Missouri Pacific) and Santa Fe–Roscoe to Snyder, Texas, 30.4 miles. But mergers among the big fellows and the closing of gateways would extinguish RS&P's raison d'être. West of Roscoe, October 17, 1981.

Tiny Texas South–Eastern for many years provided an important stream of business to Southern Pacific at Diboll in East Texas. This day in August 1985, the interchange was a bit thin.

In the wake of Rock Island's demise, newcomer Texas Northwestern Railway appeared to pick up a small crumb of former Rock Island mileage in the Texas Panhandle, using Santa Fe at Etter as its sole connecting outlet. Gruver, August 17, 1986.

IC's train 676, long an institution on the Iowa Division, offered expedited freight service out of Sioux City late every afternoon. Trying to outrun a setting sun at Marcus. May 1972.

BY THE 1970S, RAILROADS WERE A "MATURE INDUS-try." It was not a term of endearment. Indeed, many observers were ready to write off the industry, consigning it – soon, they said – to the dustbin of history. The naysayers got it wrong, happy to say, but the long decade of the 1970s proved wrenching in the extreme for those who held affection for the industry at large, for the individual companies, for the trains they ran, and for the employees who worked for them. It would be a grim ten years. Yes, there was a glimmer of hope, and a new era beckoned. It would be a hard slog getting there, but over the next several years, a very different industry would emerge – slimmed down, deregulated, and led by a talented and innovative management cadre. A new era, to be sure, one that resembled the past only at the margins.

IC for years was Iowa's premier handler of packing-house products, but reflecting a broad pattern, billings slipped in the 1970s as packers relocated their plants and as they increasingly turned to trucks for their transportation needs. Six days a week, however, IC in August 1976 still wheeled tonnage eastward from John Morell's huge facility at Sioux Falls, South Dakota. Train 776, shown here slipping through Matlock in northwest Iowa, would hand off most of its consist to train 676 from Sioux City at Cherokee.

The era of passenger-train operation by most of the country's investor-owned railroads would end on May 1, 1971 with the advent of Amtrak, a national network that would be an abbreviated model. Not included would be Illinois Central's *Hawkeye,* serving communities in the Chicago–Sioux City corridor. Truth be told, demand for its services had waned. Gone were its diner–lounge, sleepers, and head-end cars filled with mail, express, and baggage. With the sun rising and on time at 6:11 AM, no. 11 pauses in its westbound sojourn at Storm Lake, Iowa, on March 22, 1971. Yes, the conductor held the train long enough for this image to be made.

256

The Iowa Great Lakes in the northwest corner of the state represented a "prairie oasis" and predictably became a great attraction for vacationers. Indeed, a Rock Island predecessor and Milwaukee Road both tapped the area to boost discretionary travel. Each at one time sponsored steamboat operation on the lakes to move tourists from depots to hotels and lodges. All of that was in the past, but locals still perked up at the "drawbridge" separating East Lake Okoboji and West Lake Okoboji when Milwaukee ran its "as-needed" trains north from Spencer to Spirit Lake. August 1971.

Handing up messages and train orders to the head end and hind end was a routine of long duration for agents and operators. It was not much of a challenge with slow moving trains in daylight, but it took real fortitude to stand near tie-ends for this performance serving high-speed trains in the dead of night. No problem this day for the Milwaukee Road agent at Sheldon, Iowa, who has messages for this eastbound drag about to cross the Omaha (C&NW) diamond. In the background at right is Thill's Lunch Room, a Sheldon institution where once passengers, railroaders, and locals alike happened by for "a cup of java and a sinker" (coffee and doughnut) or a quick sandwich or piece of pie. July 1976.

Milwaukee Road favored on-line manufacturer Fairbanks Morse with orders for road power and a swarm of switchers like H-12–44 742 shuffling cars at Marquette, Iowa, in July 1976.

A trio of Milwaukee Road EMD SD-7s bustle westbound freight on C&NW trackage (operating rights) west of Fairmont, Minnesota. August 9, 1976.

The cumulative effects of Milwaukee Road's deferred maintenance are on full display at Emmetsburg, Iowa, this bright August morning in 1977 when a collection of cab units wheeze through town with eastbound tonnage.

The Burlington Northern (BN) merger was already two years old, but this southbound BN local at Wever, Iowa, on May 15, 1972, gave proud evidence of its CB&Q background. Wever is between Burlington and Fort Madison.

Lonely country. BN (Colorado & Southern) Extra 6912 West shoulders tonnage upgrade on the high plains near Mount Dora, New Mexico. April 1977.

Local trains meeting the needs of local customers had been a staple of American railroad practice since the inception of the industry. But shipper demands and railroad practice were evolving – changing, and changing ever so greatly – in the 1970s. The statuses of branches, secondary routes, and even entire railroad corporations were in question. Local service would reflect all of this in one way or another. This BN peddler is west of Strang, in south-central Nebraska, on the Beatrice–Holdrege line. March 8, 1978.

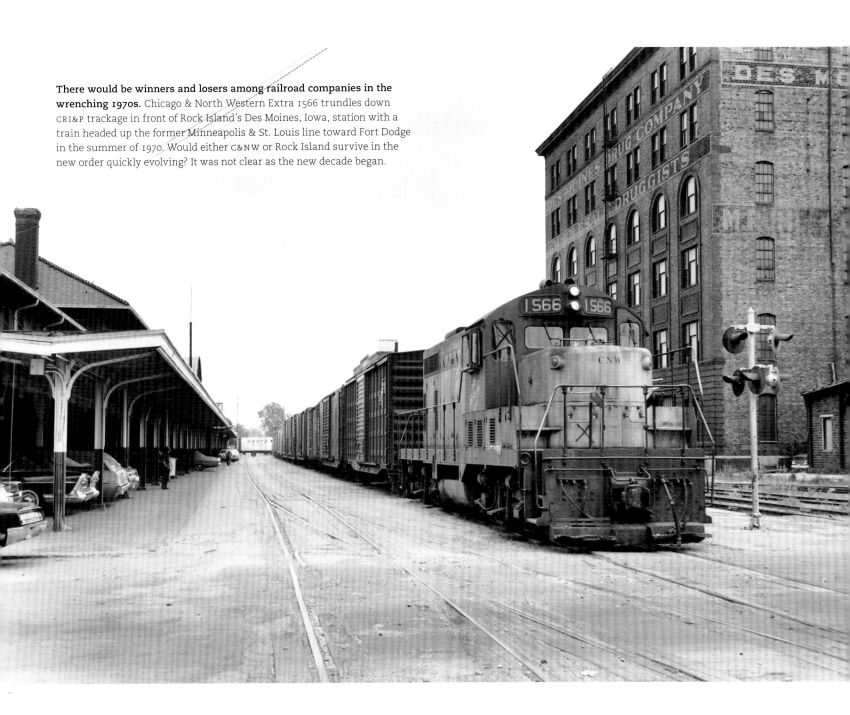

There would be winners and losers among railroad companies in the wrenching 1970s. Chicago & North Western Extra 1566 trundles down CRI&P trackage in front of Rock Island's Des Moines, Iowa, station with a train headed up the former Minneapolis & St. Louis line toward Fort Dodge in the summer of 1970. Would either C&NW or Rock Island survive in the new order quickly evolving? It was not clear as the new decade began.

**Sioux Rapids, in northwest Iowa, once had been
a crew-change point for c&nw, but no more.**
Indeed, on this day in May 1972, an eastbound
local did not even bother to stop there.

That others might live. C&NW workmen at Huron, South Dakota, on May 25, 1972, carve up an Alco, discarding much of it for scrap but saving specific elements to keep the company's remaining fleet of Alco power patched and running.

C&NW assigned considerable of its Alco power on the Winona, Minnesota–Rapid City, South Dakota, route during the 1970s. Much of it congregated at Waseca, Minnesota, at the engine terminal or on trains entering or departing. August 1977.

C&NW branch lines blanketed the entirety of its sprawling system.
Management focused on three main goals: A) Keeping Union Pacific happy
with C&NW's Chicago–Council Bluffs service; B) Getting out of the expensive Chicago commuter business; and C) Dumping as many branches as
possible. The latter goal understandably caused considerable indigestion
in much of the rural Midwest. Which of its branches would be shed?
This one through Bricelyn, Minnesota? The jury was out. Summer 1977.

Prospects for the former M&StL line in Minnesota through Sherburn were grim, with the line already sundered in two locations to the north and service offered only irregularly between St. James, Minnesota, and Estherville, Iowa. Extra 1675 has only two loads for Estherville on this trip in the late summer of 1977. The brakeman soon will be obliged to open the gate at the Milwaukee Road crossing to facilitate any further progress. The sun was setting not just on this day but also on the line itself.

AT&SF covered wagons assigned to this eastbound freight on the windswept high plains of the Oklahoma Panhandle pause at Keyes, not far from the famed Santa Fe Trail. Until recent years, Keyes had been a prime loading point for cattle, but more recently, helium was loaded nearby. July 1972.

The Budweiser distributor at Spencer, Iowa, long had been a loyal M&StL and then c&nw customer (see the Manufacturers' Railway box from St. Louis on the point), but that regular stream of business was about to disappear. c&nw then could count primarily on grain movements, corn especially. Yet track conditions on much of the line to Fort Dodge would not support the weight of covered hoppers, and terminal elevators and processors increasingly refused delivery of grain in boxcars. Rolling through verdant fields of corn between Ruthven and Ayshire and approaching grain elevators at Curlew. Summer 1977.

Kiowa, Kansas, was a vibrant railroad center served by AT&SF's busy Chicago–Los Angeles freight main as well as a secondary route feeding traffic to and from Enid, Oklahoma, and Santa Fe's "Orient" line to San Angelo, Texas. This train has just come up the Enid District. July 1972.

This station scene at Burlington, Kansas, could have been replicated endlessly across the "grain belt" of the United States and Canada. Summer 1973.

Power configurations changed startlingly as carriers purchased second-generation diesel–electric locomotives. Units once utilized on main-line trains found new homes on secondary routes or branches. Such was the case for Santa Fe's 327, heading this job at Cherokee, Oklahoma, twenty miles southwest of Kiowa, Kansas, where Guthrie and Orient lines split–converge. July 1973.

Altus, Oklahoma, was a crew-change
point for Santa Fe on its Orient route.
To left is Missouri–Kansas–Texas's
Northwestern District Yard. June 19, 1978.

OFF THE MAIN LINES

A solitary boxcar is the freight consist of Rock Island's Extra 1250 East passing through Orleans, Iowa, very near what once had been the celebrated Hotel Orleans, built and operated by Rock Island predecessor Burlington, Cedar Rapids & Northern and a fine spa and watering hole greatly applauded by wealthy nabobs during the "Gay Nineties." August 1972.

Rock Island's Extra 1325 rumbles over a steel bridge and pokes through underbrush west of Altamont, Missouri, with tonnage bound for St. Joseph. July 29, 1972.

Rock Island owned a crucial vertical artery across Oklahoma that, when connected to the rest of its system, presented a route from Chicago, Minneapolis, and St. Paul all the way to the Texas Gulf Coast. From it and from its Choctaw Route that spanned the Sooner State from east to west spewed forth a series of feeders like that serving Okeene, where a large flour mill offered significant revenue. July 1973.

Ponca City, Oklahoma, was at the end of an important fifty-five-mile branch from Enid, the latter city boasting a significant collection of towering terminal elevators, among other important customers. Power and classic Rock Island outside-frame caboose sun themselves in front of Ponca City's handsome depot. July 1973.

Built for the ages by a company that expected to live through the ages, Rock Island's station structure at Estherville, Iowa, once had housed division officers who oversaw CRI&P's affairs in northwest Iowa and eastern South Dakota. In August 1976, the local customer base yet warranted a switch job six days per week.

Sentinel at its assigned post. No snow at Limon, Colorado, this sparkling day in October 1976, but hard days of winter are in the offing. Then this Rock Island plow will be summoned from its slumber.

Everything in good order, right? Bent and beaten pilot plows on units 1345 and 1346 at the Estherville, Iowa, engine facility say otherwise. By the summer of 1979, Rock Island track conditions across much of the system ranged from tolerable to deplorable, a reflection of extended financial anemia.

A perfect metaphor for Rock Island's financial circumstance in August 1977 was the unused and dilapidated depot at Wallingford, Iowa.

Rock Island in August 1977 yet moved substantial grain tonnage in boxcars, in part because track structure on many of its primary grain-producing lines could not tolerate heavily laden covered hopper cars. Two units lead a lengthy train of empty boxes out of Estherville to be distributed to grain elevators en route to Iowa Falls. August 1977.

This EMD product in new "Rock" colors has gathered up more than a dozen boxcars loaded with new-crop wheat on Oklahoma's Mangum branch. East of Lone Wolf, headed for Anadarko and Chicasha. June 19, 1978.

Rock Island started several locals from Chicasha, Oklahoma: out to Mangum; down the loop to Anadarko, Lawton, and Waurika; and to the rock quarries at Richards Spur, where this caboose hop takes a snooze. Spring 1979.

Duluth, Winnipeg & Pacific (DW&P) provided owner Canadian National (CN) with an arrow into the central United States with a 170-mile appendage from International Falls, Minnesota, to Duluth, where connection was made with several other carriers. DW&P for much of its life was a sleepy creature, but in later years with greatly increased traffic, it would take on vital strategic importance for CN. DW&P's vest-pocket terminal in West Duluth soon would give way to a large, modern facility elsewhere. July 1976.

Soo Line focused several lines on Duluth, Minnesota, and Superior, Wisconsin, and predictably for many years was a primary player at the Twin Ports. Soo was especially important in moving prodigious amounts of grain from the west to huge lakeside terminal elevators. An assortment of power on this hauler up from Moose Lake enters the yard at Superior. July 1976.

Green Bay & Western (GB&W) advertised itself as the "Short Route between East and West" by handling tonnage to and from Lake Michigan car ferries at Kewaunee, Wisconsin. The operation certainly did reduce transit time, and it reduced per diem charges on equipment for billings that otherwise would have moved via traffic-congested Chicago. Not surprisingly, on-line customers, particularly at Green Bay, and others off-line to the west favored GB&W's strict attention to expeditious handling of their lading. Exchanging cars with Ann Arbor's *Viking* at Kewaunee, July 1977.

St. Louis–San Francisco (Frisco) and Santa Fe in 1973 had agreed to move their cross-country interchange from Floydada, Texas, to Avard, Oklahoma, but on some days Frisco still handled handsome tonnage eastbound from Quanah, Texas; local customers plus interchange from Quanah, Acme & Pacific and Fort Worth & Denver–BN. Heading down into the valley of the Red River near Carnes, Texas, March 1976.

Crossing the Red River and boring into the Sooner State with eastbound billings headed for Oklahoma City and beyond. Frisco train 3310, July 1976.

SL–SF train 3310 had a bit of switching to do at Altus, Oklahoma, on December 18, 1980. Actually, it was not a Frisco train at all, but rather Burlington Northern, because the latter had acquired Frisco a few days earlier on November 21, 1980. It was the latest chapter in a continuous stream of mergers – change fostering change fostering even more change.

Milwaukee Road, like Rock Island, was among the nation's sick carriers. It struggled to survive by jettisoning huge chunks of its route structure, but in the end it would lose its independent standing. As track structure deteriorated, more power was required to lug tonnage. This, of course, increased operating costs. It was a vicious cycle. Rumbling eastward through Ruthven, Iowa. July 1980.

Toledo, Peoria & Western (TP&W) owned a long and complicated history. In later years, it served as an important bridge road linking Pennsylvania Railroad on the east with Santa Fe on the west. At one point, TP&W ran through to Fort Madison, Iowa, with trackage rights on AT&SF from Lomax, Illinois. TP&W power laying over at Fort Madison (Shopton) before returning to Peoria and the east. July 30, 1980.

Robert E. McMillan, TP&W's president, left, shares a Santa Fe antecedent with John W. Barriger IV, assistant to the president at AT&SF. East Peoria, Illinois, March 10, 1983.

A brace of brightly colored and nicely scrubbed TP&W units tugs at a heavy train departing East Peoria, Illinois. March 11, 1983.

Seven husky six-axle units have been called out by Northwestern Pacific to lug heavy lading mostly from shippers at the upper end of its Northern California line. Virtually all of the consist will be handed off to parent Southern Pacific for further handling. Willits, May 25, 1982.

Chicago & North Western sold its Sioux Falls trackage and a few miles of main line to Ellis & Eastern, which continued to serve local customers. June 22, 1990.

AROUND THE HORN

WHAT GOES AROUND COMES AROUND. WELL, PRETTY close, but not quite in this case. The odyssey had begun in Iowa but would end in Minnesota – again, and by way of South Dakota. A change of jobs predictably explains new locations.

The allure of railroads and railroading had not escaped or evaporated, but the railroad landscape certainly had changed over the years. The number of Class One carriers had diminished to a handful. Gone were electric-trolley roads, steam, gas–electric cars, cabooses, most passenger trains, local station agencies, a host of branches and even secondary routes, and, of course, the wonderful employees who had been a part of them. "Off the main lines" became increasingly problematic. And favored cameras began to fail. Exposures became less frequent. But what a show it had been!

Sioux Falls, South Dakota, once had been a major hub of railroad activity offered by Milwaukee Road, Great Northern, Omaha, Illinois Central, and Rock Island. By 1987, much had changed. Rock Island left the city before its corporate demise, and IC followed. Milwaukee had been acquired by Soo Line, but its former assets at Sioux Falls were now the property of still others. Great Northern had become an integral part of Burlington Northern, but the line to Yankton was gone. Omaha had been fully absorbed into Chicago & North Western, but C&NW had become intent on disposing of branches and would soon exit. Extra 4284 East is about to cross Burlington Northern's Willmar–Sioux City line at Manley, Minnesota. August 30, 1988.

Burlington Northern predecessors completed a route from Willmar, Minnesota, to Sioux City, Iowa, that for most of its existence went essentially unremarked, but its strategic value under BN and its Burlington Northern Santa Fe successor was to be greatly exploited. Five big units were required to tote this heavy southbound freight by the depot at Sioux Center, Iowa, on September 30, 1990.

A short-line movement blossomed in the wake of deceased railroads, mergers, abandonments, and deregulation. One of the new entrants, Dakota & Iowa (D&I) picked up former Milwaukee Road trackage from Dell Rapids through Sioux Falls to Sioux City, moving heavy tonnage in aggregates and delighting on-line grain shippers who otherwise would have lost service. A short local putters through Akron, Iowa, on July 29, 1988.

D&I could rely on significant shipment of crushed granite from near Dell Rapids, South Dakota, much of it eagerly sought by major carriers as high-quality ballast. Power and cabooses await a call at Dell Rapids, June 24, 1990.

Duluth, Winnipeg & Pacific in later years took on a much greater strategic importance for its Canadian National owner. A new, modern terminal at the Head of the Lakes (Pokegama, Wisconsin) reflected as much. DW&P was a "hook-and-haul" operation with scant local business, but "Peg" employees fully embraced the road's "Delivered with Pride" motto. July 18, 1990.

Central Vermont (CV) was another American appendage of Canadian National. CV owned a lengthy, interesting, and complex history, but unlike its maturing view of DW&P, CN was hard pressed to determine the strategic importance of its New England route, and local billings were problematic. At least there was "light at the end of the tunnel" at Bellows Falls, Vermont, on May 24, 1989.

CN's properties in the United States were collected under the Grand Trunk Corporation (GTC) umbrella, with American managers given considerable latitude in the various operations. The St. Albans, Vermont, engine house as seen through the windshield of a CV hi-rail vehicle. May 24, 1989.

Central Vermont in an earlier era had forged traffic agreements
with steamship companies to move passengers beyond New
London, Connecticut, and it also had its own "steamer line"
for freight service to New York. New London, May 25, 1989.

OFF THE MAIN LINES

cv's Chris Burger and Tom Fawcett, left and center, confer with Amtrak's James Larson about Amtrak operations over cv. St. Albans, June 7, 1990.

In addition to cv, which was part of the GTC package, CN featured an additional historic artery in New England linking Montreal with Portland, Maine – this one not part of GTC. Waiting for a call at Island Pond, Vermont, May 29, 1991.

Canadian Pacific, too, had a presence in New England railroad circles. Hurrying Montreal-bound tonnage near Newport Center and Stevens Mill, Vermont. May 29, 1991.

Burlington Northern grain-marketing forces expended great
energy and had great success in building up unit-train grain movements from shippers on its Willmar–Sioux City route. Racing
southward near Pipestone, Minnesota, December 30, 1990.

Santa trains have been a feature at many railroads over the years. BN's entry at St. Cloud, Minnesota, in 1991 delighted local citizens and then headed off on what once had been a through route to Willmar, later stubbed at Richmond. Westbound near Rockville, December 14, 1991.

Twin Cities & Western eventually came to own and operate a portion of Milwaukee Road's route west from Minneapolis. It proved to be an efficient and innovative enterprise, much to the satisfaction of on-line customers. Westbound west of Brownton, Minnesota. August 2009.

A number of significant short lines or regional roads emerged from the ashes or discards of others as the railroad industry sorted itself out in the last quarter of the twentieth century. One of these was Dakota, Minnesota & Eastern (DM&E), which, with its Iowa, Chicago & Eastern (IC&E) corporate cousin, came to operate large chunks of what once had been part of C&NW and Milwaukee Road trackage. Ironically, both DM&E and IC&E would themselves become integral parts of much larger Canadian Pacific. New Ulm, Minnesota, was a busy place for DM&E on June 19, 2007.

A hot, humid day greets a well-powered IC&E westbound drag at Rudd, Iowa, on August 5, 2009.

Yet another striking success story in Midwestern railroad circles was Iowa Interstate, which took the death rattle out of Rock Island trackage in Illinois and Iowa. That company's well-earned self-respect was on full display at Rock Island, Illinois, August 17, 2009 – new muscular power in arrestingly bold livery.

Athearn, Robert G. *Rebel of the Rockies: A History of the Denver & Rio Grande Western Railroad.* New Haven, Conn.: Yale University Press, 1962.

Bryant, Keith L. *History of the Atchison, Topeka & Santa Fe Railway.* New York: Macmillan, 1974.

Carlson, Norman, ed. *Iowa Trolleys.* Chicago: Central Electric Railfans' Association, 1975.

Casey, Robert J., and W. A. S. Douglas. *Pioneer Railroad: The Story of the Chicago & North Western System.* New York: McGraw-Hill, 1948.

Corliss, Carlton J. *Main Line of Mid-America: The Story of the Illinois Central.* New York: Creative Age Press, 1950.

Derleth, August. *The Milwaukee Road: Its First Hundred Years.* New York: Creative Age Press, 1948.

Donovan, Frank P., Jr. *Mileposts on the Prairie: The Story of the Minneapolis & St. Louis Railway.* New York: Simmons-Boardman, 1950.

George, Preston, and Sylvan R. Wood. "The Railroads of Oklahoma." *The Bulletin*, no. 60, Railway & Locomotive Historical Society, 1943.

Grant, H. Roger. *The Corn Belt Route: A History of the Chicago Great Western Railroad Company.* DeKalb: Northern Illinois University Press, 1984.

———. *The North Western: A History of the Chicago & North Western Railway System.* DeKalb: Northern Illinois University Press, 1996.

———. *Follow the Flag: A History of the Wabash Railroad Company.* DeKalb: Northern Illinois University Press, 2009.

Hayes, William Edward. *Iron Road to Empire: The History of the Rock Island Lines.* New York: Simmons-Boardman, 1953.

Hidy, Ralph W., Muriel E. Hidy, Roy V. Scott, and Don L. Hofsommer. *The Great Northern Railway: A History.* Boston: Harvard University Business School Press, 1988.

Hilton, George W. *American Narrow Gauge Railroads.* Stanford: Stanford University Press, 1990.

Hilton, George W., and John F. Due. *Electric Interurban Railways in America.* Stanford: Stanford University Press, 1960.

Hofsommer, Don L. *Prairie Oasis: The Railroads, Steamboats, and Resorts of Iowa's Spirit Lake Country.* Des Moines, Iowa: Waukon & Mississippi Press, 1975.

———. *Katy Northwest: The Story of a Branch Line Railroad.* Boulder, Colo.: Pruett Press, 1976.

———. *The Quanah Route: A History of the Quanah, Acme & Pacific Railway.* College Station: Texas A&M University Press, 1991.

———. *Grand Trunk Corporation: Canadian National Railways in the United States, 1971–1992.* East Lansing: Michigan State University Press, 1995.

———. *The Tootin' Louis: A History of the Minneapolis & St. Louis Railway.* Minneapolis: University of Minnesota Press, 2004.

———. *Steel Trails of Hawkeyeland: Iowa's Railroad Experience.* Bloomington: Indiana University Press, 2005.

Hofsommer, Don L., ed. *Railroads in Oklahoma.* Oklahoma City: Oklahoma Historical Society, 1977.

Keilty, Edmund. *Doodlebug Country: The Rail Motor Car on the Class I Railroads of the United States.* Glendale, Calif.: Interurbans, 1982.

Klein, Maury. *Union Pacific: The Rebirth, 1894–1969.* Garden City, N.Y.: Doubleday, 1989.

Long, Bryant A., and William J. Dennis. *Mail by Rail: The Story of the Postal Transportation Service.* New York: Simmons-Boardman, 1951.

Marshall, James. *Santa Fe: The Railroad That Built an Empire.* New York: Random House, 1945.

Masterson, V. V. *The Katy Railroad and the Last Frontier.* Norman: University of Oklahoma Press, 1952.

Middleton, William D. *The Interurban Era.* Milwaukee, Wis.: Kalmbach Publishing, 1961.

Middleton, William D., George M. Smerk, and Roberta L. Diehl. *Encyclopedia of North American Railroads.* Bloomington: Indiana University Press, 2007.

Overton, Richard C. *Gulf to Rockies: The Heritage of the Fort Worth & Denver–Colorado & Southern Railways, 1861–1898.* Austin: University of Texas Press, 1953.

———. *Burlington Route: A History of the Burlington Lines.* New York: Alfred A. Knopf, 1965.

Prosser, Richard S. *Rails to the North Star: One Hundred Years of Railroad Evolution in Minnesota.* Minneapolis, Minn.: Dillon Press, 1966.

Reed, St. Clair Griffin. *A History of the Texas Railroads and of Transportation Conditions under Spain and Mexico and the Republic and the State.* Houston: The St. Clair Publishing Co., 1941.

Stover, John F. *The Life and Decline of the American Railroad.* New York: Oxford University Press, 1970.

———. *History of the Illinois Central Railroad.* New York: Macmillan, 1975.

Saunders, Richard. *Merging Lines: American Railroads, 1900–1970.* DeKalb: Northern Illinois University Press, 2001.

Waters, L. L. *Steel Trails to Santa Fe.* Lawrence: University of Kansas Press, 1950.

INDEX

BOOKS IN THE RAILROADS PAST & PRESENT SERIES

DON L. HOFSOMMER is Professor of History at St. Cloud State University and has written extensively on the history of the North American railroad industry. He is author of *Katy Northwest: The Story of a Branch Line Railroad; Steel Trails of Hawkeyeland: Iowa's Railroad Experience;* and (with H. Roger Grant) of *Iowa's Railroads: An Album.*